BEHOLD YOUR KING!

Other Books by Richard Holloway:

Let God Arise (Mowbrays 1972)

New Vision of Glory (Mowbrays 1974)

A New Heaven (Mowbrays 1979)

Beyond Belief (Mowbrays 1981)

Signs of Glory (Darton, Longman & Todd 1982)

The Killing (Darton, Longman & Todd 1984)
(Winner of the Winifred Mary Stanford Award)

The Anglican Tradition (Editor) (Mowbrays 1984)

Paradoxes of Christian Faith and Life (Mowbrays 1984)

The Sidelong Glance (Darton, Longman & Todd 1985)

The Way of the Cross (Collins 1986)
(The Archbishop of Canterbury's Lent Book)

Seven to Flee, Seven to Follow (Mowbrays 1986)

Crossfire: Faith and Doubt in an Age of Certainty (Collins 1988)

The Divine Risk (Editor) (Darton, Longman & Todd 1990)

Another Country, Another King (Collins 1991)

Who Needs Feminism? (SPCK 1991)

Anger, Sex, Doubt and Death (SPCK 1992)

The Stranger in the Wings (SPCK 1994)

RICHARD HOLLOWAY

BEHOLD · YOUR · KING!

Meditations on the Death
and Resurrection of
Christ

FOR TONY AND JEANNIE WHATMOUGH

First published in Great Britain 1995
Society for Promoting Christian Knowledge
Holy Trinity Church
Marylebone Road
London NW1 4DU

Chapters 1 to 14 originally published under the title *The Killing: Meditations on the Death of Christ* (London: Darton, Longman & Todd, 1984) © D, L & T 1984.

'Musée des Beaux Arts' from *Collected Shorter Poems 1927–1957* by W. H. Auden, © Faber and Faber Ltd. Reprinted with permission of the publisher.

'Burnt Norton' from *Collected Poems 1909–1962* by T. S. Eliot, © Faber and Faber Ltd. Reprinted with permission of the publisher.

Glass and Stone by Katherine Charnley, © of the author. Reprinted with permission.

Scripture quotations from the Revised Standard Version of the Bible, copyright 1946, 1952, 1971 by the Division of Christian Education of the National Council of the Churches of Christ in the USA. Used by permission.

Extracts from the Authorised Version of the Bible (the King James Bible), the rights in which are vested in the Crown, are reproduced by permission of the Crown's Patentee, Cambridge University Press.

British Library Cataloguing-in-Publication Data
A catalogue record for this book is available from the British Library

ISBN 0-281-04811-8

Typeset by Action Typesetting Ltd., Gloucester
Printed in Great Britain by
BPC Paperbacks Ltd
Member of the British Printing Co. Ltd.

Contents

Prologue

On Good Friday 1954, I determined to convert my father. Good Friday at Kelham Theological College, where I was a student, was a rigorous day, spent mostly in Chapel. The Three Hours ended at 3 o'clock, and we broke our fast with a simple meal at 4. It was during a solitary walk before tea that I resolved to write to my father. I can't remember a thing about it now, but the Three Hours devotion had touched me deeply. I can, however, remember my subsequent train of thought. As I walked the quiet roads away from Kelham's front gate I heard the rumble of lorries on the Great North Road, driving south to London or north to Scotland, and I was surprised and offended by them. I mourned the fact that our Lord was dead and the world paid no attention. Years later I would learn from W. H. Auden that this is how it always is. The mourners are transfixed by their tragedy, but the world goes on as usual.

> About suffering they were never wrong,
> The Old Masters: how well they understood
> Its human position; how it takes place
> While someone else is eating or opening a
>   window or just walking dully along;
> How, when the aged are reverently,
>   passionately waiting

For the miraculous birth, there always must
  be
Children who did not specially want it to
  happen, skating
On a pond at the edge of the wood:
They never forgot
That even the dreadful martyrdom must run
  its course
Anyhow in a corner, some untidy spot
Where the dogs go on with their doggy life
  and the torturer's horse
Scratches its innocent behind on a tree.

('Musée des Beaux Arts':
Collected Shorter Poems 1927–1957)

Knowing better than Christ, I wanted to protect him from his own passion for obscurity and call the world to attention. Though I could not stop the traffic on the Great North Road, maybe I could call my father to repentance. I went back to my room and wrote to him. With italicized self-consciousness, I told him that Jesus had died for him. If he went to confession and took Jesus into his heart his life would be transformed. The person to whom this evangelical epistle went was a small, quiet man, who spent eighty hours a week labouring in a dye works. Like many working men, he was uncomfortable in church and embarrassed by religious discussion. He had the supreme tact never to refer to my letter. When my mother died twenty years later, I found it in her sideboard drawer and blushed when I read it. My mistake was to see the death of Jesus as an ecclesiastical event, something that belonged to the Church, not the world.

Turning the death of Jesus into a religious rather than a human event has predictable consequences. People who are uncomfortable with the Church lose Jesus, because the stealers of his body control access to him. The one who died to break down walls of partition is taken to a private cemetery where visitors are expected to pay a stiff entrance fee. It's an ancient human tradition to charge children for bread their father has provided, so it is not surprising that it happens with spiritual as well as natural resources. It is robbery, nevertheless. Jesus belongs to the world, not to the Church. He died for all, not for a few. He was already close to the lorry drivers on the Great North Road. He was closer to my father, running endless bales of cloth through steaming red dye in a freezing and dilapidated factory, than he was to me in my spiritual exaltation in Kelham Chapel. Maybe it's sad that the lorry driver and the dye man don't know what Jesus has done for them, but it doesn't really matter. What *does* matter is that we try to make them pay for what was freely given.

It's the grace of the crucifixion that increasingly speaks to me. God does not demand war reparations for this crime. Christ lays it not to our charge. The crucifixion is an act of forgiveness in which God's grace runs ahead of human cruelty. Characteristically, it is Luke who best captures this aspect of the Passion, by recording a look and a phrase. Of all the characters in the Passion, it is Peter I most identify with. Peter was a great talker, who rarely measured his words. He shot from the lip, embarrassing himself and those who loved him with streams of unhelpful verbiage. He blustered on the Holy Mount about building tabernacles for Jesus and his heavenly guests, when he should have kept silence. He boasted and bumbled his way through our Lord's ministry, getting most things wrong, not least the steadiness of his own courage and commitment. Words have always been a great trap for Christian ministers. Constantly called upon to speak, they either say too much or too little, go too far or not far enough, put things too bluntly or too smoothly; and they bring wrath and derision upon their own heads. Some of them learn Benjamin Jowett's law, 'Never explain, never apologize, never make the same mistake twice', but others endlessly try to unsay what they have too clearly said, or to undo what they have too publicly done. We live by words and die by them, enduring death by a thousand qualifications.

In his Passion our Lord does two things with our words. After Peter's bitter denial, Luke writes the most poignant sentence in Scripture: 'And the Lord turned and looked at Peter.' It was a look that made Peter weep bitterly, because it was a look of pity. Jesus understood the generosity as well as the instability that lay behind Peter's words. Inner uncertainty can make our language harsher than we feel. The world's contempt can trip us into desperate speech, but Christ 'knoweth whereof we are made'. He turns and looks at us as we go on and on till our words turn into tears. In the Passion narrative Peter's undisciplined babbling is counterpointed by our Lord's concentrated silence. Silence gathers at the heart of the Passion. For all the difference in detail, each of the accounts conveys a sense of profound silence at the centre of the action, a silence that is redemptive. In the Church the movement is usually the other way: we bind people by our words rather than free them by the graciousness of our silence. Just occasionally, not often enough, we feel the Lord looking at us; our words falter, stop, and the false words become honest tears.

It is Luke who makes explicit the divine forgiveness at the heart of the Passion. The moment of the nailing, the precise centre of the lawless act, is also the moment of absolution: 'Father forgive them; for they know not what they do.' God's grace is coactive with human sin; the moment of human theft is the moment of divine gift. The same event is both our loss and our salvation, our mourning and our joy. The Russian poet Osip Mandelstam said that it was not the Church's task to redeem the world. That has already been taken care of. It is our happy responsibility to proclaim the fact, to tell Jerusalem that her warfare is accomplished. Too often we get the news wrong, preaching as though all is yet to fight for, as though the victory were in doubt. Our news is that the war is over, our reconciliation achieved. That would be good news if we believed it. Our tragedy is that the Church contradicts the liberality of God, by trying to get the world to pay a religious duty on what has been so freely given. The Church is not the gospel but it ought to be its news agency, here to announce what another has won.

I am glad now I did not succeed in converting my father in 1954, but I am sorry I did not find a way of sharing with him the joy of our liberation in Christ, though I suspect he already knew it. When he died a few years ago we did not bring his body into church for the funeral. We left him in the hearse outside the church where he was more comfortable – outside with Jesus.

I have thought of him often as I prepared this new and expanded edition of this book. Preaching the cross is one of the most taxing and privileged responsibilities of the Christian minister. It is one I rarely accomplish without weeping. I offer this book as a prayer to the Divine Outsider on behalf of all the other outsiders for whom he died.

PART 1

THE ACTORS

1 · *The Secret Admirer*

When Jesus had spoken these words, he went
forth with his disciples across the Kidron valley,
where there was a garden which he and his disciples entered.

(John 18.1, RSV)

There is a notorious newspaper in Britain which
advertises itself with the slogan: 'All life is there.'
I do not want to say anything about the quality
of the newspaper, but I think it is a good slogan, and I would like to borrow it. What is
more, I would like to use it as a motto for
the New Testament: All life is *there*. The New
Testament is about Jesus Christ and how people
reacted to him, what they made of him, what
they did to him. But Jesus Christ is not just a
character from history, someone in the past about
whom we read. 'Jesus Christ is the same, yesterday, today and for ever', says the letter to the
Hebrews. Now, I obviously cannot persuade you
of that fact. I cannot argue you into accepting
it. But I do not have to. If Jesus Christ is as alive
today as he was then, then he is just as able now
as he was then to make himself known to people,
to confront them, challenge them to follow him,
be rejected by them. In short, everything that happened then still happens. So what we get in the
New Testament is not a few pages of history, but
a description of what is still happening. He still

walks our streets. He still comes in and out of our lives. Here he is still worshipped, there he is still rejected. Still he challenges us, and still his challenge goes unheeded. He crouches still in our doorways, and is raised up in crosses at every street corner. And he still rises from all the deaths we subject him to. The one thing he won't do is go away and leave us alone. He will not let us forget him. Nor will he pressurize us into going to him, though he knows that only then will we find true happiness. He wants us to go to him, of course, but he wants us to *want* to go. He *bids* us, *beseeches* us; he does not command. So it is still easy to avoid him, but only for a time, because one day we shall come to him, either in life or beyond life, and we shall probably all mourn for the time we wasted or looked another way or picked up stones to cast at him. Jesus is alive, though I have often wished he were not. I have often wished he would go away and leave me alone. But he never does. He still comes to us. The New Testament is about *us*. All life is there. We are all in it. It talks about all the ways we find to deal with this Jesus who stubbornly haunts our history and who will not stay in the grave where they laid him. That is why Christians often go over the story of how they rejected him and nailed him to a cross. It is an old story, to be true, but it is absolutely up to the minute as well. It is true yesterday, today and for ever. All life is there. I am there, and so are you. There are lots of characters in the story

4

as we read it in the New Testament. Some of them have names and some of them do not. Some of them are well-known; some of them are unknown, just like us. But all life is there, and all the ways men and women react to Jesus.

I want to think, first, about someone from the story whose name we do not even know and about whom we know almost nothing. I call him the Secret Admirer. The story starts in a private garden, the Garden of Gethsemane. We must not think of it as a public park, like Hyde Park in London or Princes Street Gardens in Edinburgh. It was a private garden, which must have belonged to a wealthy person. He was a secret admirer of Jesus, and he probably put the garden at his disposal: 'Use it any time you like, go there to rest from time to time, try and get away from it all whenever you can.' We don't know how often Jesus did use it, but we do know that he spent his last night on earth there, in torment and foreboding, and it was there they arrested him in the wee small hours of the morning. Father Mackay, a former vicar of All Saints Margaret Street in London, described a visit he made to the Garden of Gethsemane in these words:

These old olive-trees, if not themselves as old as our Lord's time, may well have sprung as young shoots from the trees he knelt under.

The Paschal moon shone through the olive branches as we knelt at our prayers, and threw a

5

confused black and white pattern on the ground. The dogs of the city kept up their distant barking; noises from the streets were carried on the night wind; now and again a trumpet sounded from the citadel, awaking memories of the awful night long ago.

When they came for Jesus, there must have been quite an uproar, and it must have disturbed the sleep of all the well-off people who lived round the gardens. But none of them came out to see what was going on. They were too worldly-wise for that. They knew how to keep out of trouble. They knew it was dangerous to meddle, to 'have a go', as they say. So they shoved their heads under their pillows till the noise ceased and Jesus had been taken away. And so did the Secret Admirer. He did not intervene. He liked Jesus, admired him, but he did not want to get mixed up in it all.

I have often been a *secret* admirer of Jesus. There has never been a time in my life when I have not known about him, but there have been many times when I have kept him very definitely at a safe distance. I have not wanted to commit myself, make myself look stupid or religious or out of the ordinary. My admiration has often been very secret. Public commitment to Jesus would be more than embarrassing; it might even be painful. So I keep my head well down. I am a secret admirer. I know something important is going on, and I know I am avoiding the challenge. Inside myself I am a little ashamed, because love for Jesus is a difficult thing to keep secret. Nevertheless, I manage to keep it hidden. I am a Secret Admirer.

2 * The Traitor

> And immediately, while he was still speaking, Judas came, one of the twelve, and with him a crowd with swords and clubs, from the chief priests and the scribes and the elders. Now the betrayer had given them a sign, saying 'The one I shall kiss is the man; seize him and lead him away safely.' And when he came, he went up to him at once, and said, 'Master!' And he kissed him.
>
> (Mark 14.43–45, RSV)

Judas Iscariot! One of the cruellest riddles of history is to discover why Judas betrayed Jesus. We shall never know exactly, though there are several possible reasons.

There is an old tradition which says that Judas was the nephew of Caiaphas, the High Priest who was determined to get rid of Jesus. Judas was persuaded to become a secret agent to plot the downfall of Jesus. Whether this is true or not, it is certainly true that at the end Judas became a tool in the hands of the enemies of our Lord, and he was used to bring about his arrest.

Another explanation is that Judas did it for the money. John tells us that Judas 'was a thief and had the bag and stole from it'. Judas certainly seems to have been the treasurer of our Lord's band of disciples. If he was a thief, as John, writing long after, maintains, then it is just possible.

But neither of these explanations really produces a convincing reason for what he did. The real clue

8

probably lies in his name, 'Iscariot'. This word may be connected with the Latin word *sicarius*, a dagger-bearer, a knifer, a razorman. The sicarii were fanatical nationalists, professional revolutionaries, who believed in the violent overthrow of their Roman masters and who promptly disposed of anyone who got in their way. It is possible that Judas belonged to this company. He probably saw in Jesus the heaven-sent leader, the great charismatic figure who would unite the country against the Roman occupation. There could be two reasons for the betrayal, therefore. When Judas realized that Jesus did not plan to take the way of armed revolt, he could have betrayed him into the hands of his enemies in sheer disgust. This is the kind of thing a disappointed and embittered revolutionary might do. But even more likely is the possibility that Judas tried to force the hand of Jesus by precipitating a crisis. By placing him in a position of danger, he thought, Jesus would react violently in his own defence, and the revolution would be on. It would be the night of the long knives. Blood would flow. The kingdom would be won by violence.

Judas was probably genuinely fond of Jesus, and there are many indications in the Gospels that Jesus loved him and had great hopes for him. The kiss need not have been an act of hypocrisy. Maybe Judas saw it as a signal to revolt. 'This is it, master, the hour is here; buckle on your gun belt and come.' But, to his horror, Jesus allows himself to be taken. Only this explanation can account for what happens next. Matthew tells us:

> Then Judas, which had betrayed him, when he saw that he was condemned, repented himself, and brought again the thirty pieces of silver to the chief priests and elders, saying, I have sinned in that I have betrayed the innocent blood. And they said, What is that to us? See thou to that. And he cast down the pieces of silver in the temple, and departed, and went and hanged himself.
>
> (Matt. 27.3–5, AV)

In a moment of devastating insight Judas realizes that he has, in fact, delivered Jesus to death. In that moment he may also have realized the uselessness of the dream on which he had built his whole life – the dream of revolt, of political independence. In total despair he goes and hangs himself, and enters history as the greatest traitor of all time, the man who delivered the Son of God to death. Judas Iscariot.

Judas is not a man with whom we readily identify. We can see ourselves in Peter: those sudden enthusiasms that fade as quickly as they come and leave us more despairing and undisciplined than ever. Or we can see ourselves in Thomas, 'doubting Thomas', the man who wanted his faith constantly fortified by proof. Peter and Thomas, yes. But rarely ever Judas, except in rather rhetorical moments. And yet Judas is probably nearer to our style than these others.

The Christian religion, the Way of Jesus, is costly and painful. It imposes upon us a well-nigh impossible discipline of love: 'By this shall all men know that ye are my disciples, if ye have love one to another.' (AV) It is possible to claim to be a follower of Jesus, a member of his Church, and never allow him to challenge our selfishness, our lack of love. Like Judas, we can have Jesus on our own terms. We claim to follow him but, in fact, we try to arrange things so that he follows us or, at least, keeps out of our life.

Judas, in other words, is a person who has his own plans, his own policy, his own style, his own way of doing things, yet who claims that they are Christ's plans, Christ's way of doing things. Christ is always the exclusive possession of our club: he is a revolutionary, if that is what we believe in; or he is a conservative. He belongs to my race and my church and my group within the church. Whatever it is we believe in, Christ is on our side, backing up our action, supporting our thing.

We all have fears and prejudices, insecurities and resentments, and we use Christ, not to judge them and heal them and burn them up, but to strengthen and confirm them. We don't really follow Christ. Like Judas, we try to get him to follow us. We try to sign him on. 'Hail Master'. And we betray the Son of Man with a kiss. Judas Iscariot was the man who tried to enlist the Son of God in his private army.

That is why we ought to examine our own record from time to time. We are usually so busy organizing Christ into our own schemes that we never leave time to listen to his words and his judgements. That is why we bring all our fear and distrust to the foot of the cross; all our weakness and greed; all our hate and the things that make us bitter. But not these only. Judas' ideas were not all mean. He had a vision of a liberated Palestine and it was a noble vision. But even our noble visions have to be made captive to Christ. We have to bring to him not only our weaknesses to be judged and healed, but our strengths too. All our ideals, all the good causes we give ourselves to, have to be led behind the crucified.

Judas could have been a prince among the apostles if he had only learned to follow Christ instead of trying to lead him. Alas, I, too, am Judas Iscariot.

3 * The Onlooker

And they laid hands on him and seized him. But one of those who stood by drew his sword, and struck the slave of the high priest and cut off his ear. And Jesus said to them, 'Have you come out as against a robber, with swords and clubs to capture me? Day after day I was with you in the temple teaching, and you did not seize me. But let the scriptures be fulfilled.' And they all forsook him, and fled. And a young man followed him, with nothing but a linen cloth about his body; and they seized him, but he left the linen cloth and ran away naked.

(Mark 14.46–52, RSV)

Mark tells us that while Jesus was in the Garden of Gethsemane with his disciples, 'Judas, one of the Twelve, appeared, and with him was a crowd armed with swords and cudgels, sent by the chief priests, lawyers and elders.' Father Mackay describes the scene like this:

The men in the garden were caught in a trap. And now, in and out among the olives, with swift, unequal steps, there came the figure of a man – the most terrible figure in human history. With a quavering, 'Hail, Rabbi!' he did not merely kiss Jesus, but, overdoing his part, he covered Him with kisses.

As I have already pointed out, the whole episode must have been disconcerting to the residents of Gethsemane in the adjoining villas. We know that

13

at least one man came out to see what was happening. Our Lord's arrest must have caused quite an uproar. Some of his followers, we are told, tried to make a fight of it, and the High Priest's servant had his ear cut off before Jesus calmed things down. One young man, we know for sure, threw on his dressing gown and ventured into the garden to find out what on earth was happening at such an unearthly hour. Only Mark's Gospel mentions his presence, in what must be one of the most fascinating footnotes in history. He must have lurked behind the olive tree, watching the strange scene: the exaggerated casualness of Judas; the hysterical violence of the disciples, melting suddenly into fear as they escape through the trees; the neat, professional brutality of the temple police as they put chains on their prisoner with practised thoroughness; and the powerful and commanding dignity of our Lord at the centre of the scene. All this the young man from the neighbouring villa sees. Then a twig snaps beneath his feet, and the police discover his presence. 'There's one of them! Get hold of him, Jacob!' They lunge after the young man and grab the loose folds of his linen robe. He struggles free and runs away naked, his dressing gown in the hands of his captors. A footnote to the most momentous night in history: 'And he left the linen cloth, and fled from them naked.' Rough treatment for a mere onlooker, you may think, yet the Temple Police were better theologians than they themselves realized. We are often tempted to be spectators at the Passion, but it is not possible. We have to be on one side or the other. There can be no lurking among the olive trees as detached onlookers. But it is very tempting. Most of us, after all, live close to Gethsemane. We have been brought up in close proximity to Jesus Christ. It is difficult to avoid the knowledge that something is going on. We cannot escape the uproar, try as we do to stuff our head under the pillows. Like the young man, we are aware that something is happening. In our society it is still not quite possible to avoid Christ. We live close to Gethsemane. We cannot avoid Christ, but it is tempting just to look on. We feel at once fascinated yet repelled, by the strange man in the garden over the wall.

What is it about the Passion of Jesus Christ which so fascinates us, in spite of ourselves, in spite of our desperate attempts not to get too involved? Why are we drawn to the uproar at such odd and defenceless moments? Why can't we just stay indoors and avoid the whole unpleasant business? What are we doing here among these wretched olive trees in this strange half-light, gazing down on that uncomfortably majestic man in chains?

Well, on one level it is because executions fascinate us. We can tell much about a man by the manner of his death. Martyrdom always fascinates weaker persons. But what is so special about this martyrdom? There have been others even more dramatic. There have been many men of whom it could be said: 'Nothing in his life became him like the leaving of it.' We know more about the execution of Blessed Thomas More, and about his motives as he went to the block. We can admire the elegant courage of King Charles the Martyr, as he lifts up his long hair to prevent it obstructing the blade of the guillotine. And there have been countless others who faced death with dignity and courage. Certainly, the courage and dignity of Jesus before his accusers and executioners is compelling, but that alone does not account for the mysterious fascination of the cross. Men have not sung love songs to the guillotine or the hangman's rope. They have not hung small replicas of the electric chair round their necks or clutched them for comfort and reassurance at moments of dread and temptation, and at the moment of death. But all these things they have done to the cross: 'Faithful cross above all other, One and only noble tree'. 'When I survey the wondrous cross'. All this about an instrument of execution. There can be only two reasons for the claims which are made about the crucifixion of Jesus Christ: either there is truth in them; or Christ's death gave rise to the greatest delusion in history – the claim that this event was of universal significance. When we examine what the Church claims was happening, we can no longer remain a spectator. We must commit ourselves, either in support of the claims, because we believe they are true; or in opposition to them because we believe they are a massive and paranoid delusion which must be stamped out. We cannot be detached about this event. There can be no hanging back among the olive trees. We are either for or against him.

Tradition tells us that the young man who fled away naked was Mark himself. He puts this little story into his Gospel as a sort of signature, a remembrance of the young man who tried to hold back, to look on among the olive trees. That night he fled away naked. But he came back, later, to make his choice and to witness by his own life and death. Am I still holding back? Am I an onlooker at the Passion?

4 * The Accuser

And they led Jesus to the high priest; and all the chief priests and the elders and the scribes were assembled.... the high priest asked him, 'Are you the Christ, the Son of the Blessed?' And Jesus said, 'I am; and you will see the Son of man sitting at the right hand of Power, and coming with the clouds of heaven.' And the high priest tore his mantle, and said, 'Why do we still need witnesses? You have heard his blasphemy. What is your decision?' And they all condemned him as deserving death.

(Mark 14.53–64, RSV)

After they arrested Jesus in the Garden of Gethsemane they brought him before one of the most powerful men in Jerusalem to be tried. They brought him face to face with Caiaphas, the high priest. We do not have high priests nowadays, and church courts are not able to sentence anyone to death any longer, but we must not make the mistake of thinking that there are no Caiaphases left. There is nothing new under the sun. Everything in our story is still going on. All life is there, and Caiaphas is still here. Caiaphas was absolutely right in what he said about Jesus. He put his finger on the central problem, the matter that we have to make up our minds about. Jesus was sentenced to death for what they called blasphemy: according to the gospels, he claimed a unique identification with God; as the Fourth Gospel put it, he implied that he and God were so close that what he was

God was, and what God was he was. No wonder Caiaphas was driven nearly mad with anger and disgust. The story tells us that he tore his robe and said the man had condemned himself with his own words. No other witnesses were needed, because Jesus had, by what he said about himself, pleaded guilty to the charge. And Caiaphas was right. We cannot just leave a man like Jesus of Nazareth to his own devices. We cannot maintain an attitude of affectionate or even contemptuous neutrality to someone who makes 'himself out to be the Son of God'. We have to make a decision on an issue like that. We must take sides. We must either worship and adore him and give him our life, or condemn him as deserving death. That is the real scandal of Christianity.

The real issue is not the romantic death of an attractive man who was hard done to, but the lifting-up upon the cross of one in whom God was uniquely at work. How can we be indifferent to a claim like that, a claim that is insane in its absurdity? That is the real scandal, and it is better to be a Caiaphas, better to be an enemy of this man, than a bored and indifferent onlooker. Most people can approve of the ethical teaching of Jesus. Most people can admire the way he faced death. There is little controversy there. That is not what caused the fuss and causes it still. Noble teaching and a noble death do not scandalize people. After a while they simply bore them, and Jesus Christ was not a bore. He was either insane, 'beside himself', as his own family thought; or he was the incarnation of God's love. We must take sides on that one. He demands our allegiance or our opposition. They didn't crucify Jesus because of his politics, contrary to what many theologians claim. They didn't crucify him simply because he was a good man and most other men in Jerusalem were evil, contrary to what many preachers have claimed. They crucified him because he identified his own message with the mind and heart of God. The charge was quite specific: blasphemy of a sort that could not be tolerated; sacrilege of unbelievably momentous proportions. He told the Jews, for whom the Temple was the holiest place on earth, the indwelling of God's presence, that he, in his own person, would replace the Temple. Imagine if a man burst into your church during the service on Easter Day and shouted, 'Don't go to the altar, don't make your communion. You don't have to receive me under the forms of bread and wine, because I am here in your midst in the flesh. The shadow has departed, the reality has come. I am among you.' Since humanity has grown more tender, and blasphemy bothers us little today, we would ignore him or have him committed to a mental hospital. The Jew of our Lord's day took these things much more seriously. The penalty for this enormous blasphemy was death. To the Jew the issue was simple. We must either follow this man, acknowledge his claim, or we must put him to death. Detachment wasn't possible, nor is it possible today. There can be no hanging back among the olive trees as disinterested spectators. If what this man said of himself is true, then it concerns us whether we like it or not. We cannot escape from it.

Nowadays, we have various ways round this challenge. For example, some say that they crucified Jesus because of his politics. Well, that is not the case, though it is true they put a political angle on the charge to get the Romans to execute him, because that was the only way to achieve their purpose. (The irony is that on the very day they killed Jesus, they released a real terrorist called Barabbas in order to please the Jerusalem mob, but Jesus they delivered up to death.) Nor is it true that they killed him because he was a good man and all the other important Jews were evil. That is a terrible lie, and it has darkened the very face of history and given rise to one of the most evil forms of racism known to humanity: anti-Semitism. They crucified Jesus for blasphemy, for making a claim about himself that most people would find unacceptable. Nowadays, of course, we wouldn't execute such a man. Today we would offer him treatment or ignore him. This is the point made by Studdart Kennedy. At Golgotha, he says, men at least crucified Jesus, they responded to him with passion and strength, but –

When Jesus came to Birmingham they simply
     passed him by
They never hurt a hair of him, they simply
     let him die;
For men had grown more tender, and they
     would not give him pain,
They only just passed down the street, and
     left him in the rain.
Still Jesus cried, 'Forgive them, for they
     know not what they do',
And still it rained the wintry rain that
     drenched him through and through;
The crowds went home and left the streets
     without a soul to see,
And Jesus crouched against a wall and cried
     for Calvary.

What Caiaphas did was better, much better. It
is better to be an enemy of Jesus than to be indifferent to him, for then we are taking him
seriously. And it is still true today. We must
either surrender to this man or fight him to death.
We must respond with passion. Who can be indifferent to the claims that Christians make? Who
can hold these unbelievable facts in their mind,
and remain unaffected? Even as I recite them they
thrill and scandalize me: the everlasting Father
among us in Christ; God among us, in the dust
and tears of Galilee; God among us in the streets
of Jerusalem; God among us in the olive groves
of Gethsemane. God among us, raised high on a

cross. Who can be indifferent to these claims? Not Caiaphas, certainly; certainly not he. But what about me? Will I stand back for ever?

5 * *The Deserter*

And after a little while again the bystanders said
to Peter, 'Certainly you are one of them; for you
are a Galilean.' But he began to invoke a curse on
himself and to swear, 'I do not know this man
of whom you speak.' And immediately the cock
crowed a second time. And Peter remembered how
Jesus had said to him, 'Before the cock crows twice,
you will deny me three times.' And he broke down
and wept.

Mark 14.70–72, RSV)

All life is there. In the story of the suffering
and the death of Christ there are all sorts of
characters. We call them bit parts or walk-on
actors, who appear briefly, perform their part in
the drama, and disappear without further mention.
We never even learn their names. But there are
others with more important parts, central actors
in the unfolding events: Jesus himself, Judas, a
name dark with guilt and shame, and Caiaphas,
the vehement and articulate high priest who
brought about his death. And there is Peter.
Next to Jesus, it is Peter I love best, Peter with
whom I identify. Peter the deserter, the boastful
and impulsive; Peter the leader; Peter the man
who denied his master. His part in the story
is the most heartbreaking, and I cannot read it
without a lump in my throat. After the arrest in
the Garden of Gethsemane, Peter followed on at a
safe distance. During the trial he stood outside in

the courtyard warming himself at a fire burning in a brazier during the chill hours before dawn. There he was challenged three times by some of the onlookers and servants: 'Surely you are one of his followers?' Each time Peter denied it with an oath: 'I do not know this man.' After the third denial the cock crowed twice, signalling the end of that tormented night in the strange, seething, half-light before the break of day. Peter, we read, remembered the words of Jesus: 'Before the cock crows twice, you will deny me three times.' And he broke down and wept.

How well I know that feeling, how often I have tasted those tears of terrible regret after my own many denials of Jesus. That is why I love Peter. I love him because he was a failure, a deserter, a terribly human man who found that following Jesus was almost impossibly difficult. Peter was no hero. He was not one of these superhuman perfect Christians who make us shiver in our shoes as we contemplate their achievements, their holiness, their uprightness. We all know people like that, who make us feel judged and found wanting, consigned to the ranks of the second-class. But not Peter. Peter, like most of us, did not make a very good Christian, and the New Testament does not try to pretend otherwise. That is why it is such a marvellous book to read. All life is there, with its failures and betrayals, its tears and its great sorrows. And the tale of failure again and again features Peter.

Peter wasn't his real name. His real name was Simon. Peter was a nickname which meant rock. Jesus gave him the nickname, and it does not seem very apt, does it, for someone who crumbled again and again? Maybe there was some humour in the name. But it was just as likely that Jesus saw something in Peter that would, finally, after many failures, become firm and constant, like rock. But it took a long time, a very long time. All through his life Peter was constantly failing, making a mess of things, betraying those he loved. He failed Christ in little things, just like us. But we fail him in the big things, too, or would, if we were put to the test. Peter did. Even at a moment of supreme danger and threat to the one he loved most of all in the world, he failed. Peter misunderstood much about Jesus, and made many mistakes in trying to change Jesus into someone more acceptable to him and to others. But there was one thing he really understood about his Lord: he knew that Jesus was one who forgave sins. And not only once or twice, but *always*. That one thing he learnt, and it meant that Peter was able to keep on and on, after failure. In spite of all his failures and weaknesses, Peter was great in one thing: he never, finally, gave up. He believed in the forgiveness of sins, so he went on and on. He fell at all the fences, but he just picked himself up and struggled on, blinded with tears and covered with mire. And that was his glory. It was this quality which Jesus must have detected in him, this refusal ever to accept defeat. In his long life Peter lost all the battles, but he finally won the war.

There is a lovely legend which says that Peter was in Rome when the Emperor Nero started a savage persecution of the Church. Rome was in flames, and Peter started walking away from the terror. He set out along the Appian Way, an old man now, weary from all his journeyings for Christ, not sure what he ought to do or where he ought to go. And as he trudged away from Rome Jesus met him, going back in the direction of the city. Peter asked him the famous question: '*Quo vadis Domine?*' 'Where are you going, Lord?' 'I go to Rome to die for you', replied Jesus. Peter, we are told, stopped and turned round slowly, and this time he did not fail: he went back to Rome and death.

People like us can learn a good deal from Peter. His real secret was humility. It takes humility to struggle on in spite of repeated failure. Only the proud and self-pitying are defeated by failure. The humble, however, soon shake off the failures of the past. They never had an inflated idea of themselves in the first place. They know that they will not be judged by their successes but by their perseverance, so they pick themselves up, swallow the lump in their throat, and struggle on. That was Peter's way. According to tradition, when they came to crucify him, he asked to be crucified upside down, because he felt unworthy to die in the same position as his Lord. At the end, Peter won the war. If you, like me, are not much of a Christian, then Peter's story will give you courage. No matter what your failures are, pick yourself up and, even if tears are blinding you, do not give up the struggle.

6 * *The Politician*

So when Pilate saw that he was gaining nothing, but rather that a riot was beginning, he took water and washed his hands before the crowd, saying, 'I am innocent of this man's blood; see to it yourselves.' And all the people answered, 'His blood be on us and on our children!' Then he released ... Barabbas, and having scourged Jesus, delivered him to be crucified.

(Matt. 27.24–26, RSV)

In 'The Man Born To Be King', Dorothy L. Sayers describes the dream Claudia Procla, the wife of Pontius Pilate, had:

PILATE: Claudia, Claudia, tell me what was this dream of yours?

CLAUDIA: I was in a ship at sea, voyaging among the islands of the Aegean. At first the weather seemed calm and sunny but presently, the sky darkened and the sea began to toss with the wind ... Then out of the east, there came a cry, strange and piercing. '*Pan ho megas tethneke. Pan ho megas tethneke.*' ... And I said to the captain, 'What do they cry?' And he answered, 'Great Pan is dead.' And I asked him, 'How can God die?' And he answered, 'Don't you

29

remember? They crucified him. He suffered under Pontius Pilate.' ... Then all the people in the ship turned their faces to me and said: 'Pontius Pilate ... Pontius Pilate. He suffered under Pontius Pilate ... crucified, dead and buried ... *sub Pontio Pilato* ... Pilate ... he suffered ... suffered ... under Pontius Pilate ... under Pontius Pilate ...' in all tongues and all voices ... even the little children with their mothers ... 'suffered under *Pontio Pilato* ... *crucifié sous Ponce Pilate* ... *gekreuzigt unter Pontius Pilatus*' ... your name, husband, your name continually, 'he suffered under Pontius Pilate.'

Claudia Procla heard her husband's name sounding through the centuries. And, of course, it has. The Christian creeds have carried the message down the ages: 'Jesus Christ his only son our Lord ... suffered under Pontius Pilate, was crucified, dead, and buried.' Pontius Pilate. Why is he in the creed?

Well, the obvious answer, though not the really important one, is that the use of his name firmly fixes the crucifixion in history. We are dealing here with an event as definite as today's headlines. He was crucified under Pontius Pilate. Pontius Pilate was Governor of Judea from AD 26–36, when he was recalled to Rome. We know a fair bit about him. He showed very little understanding of the Jews whom he was sent to govern, though, to be fair, few Romans would have known how to deal with a people as obsessed with religion as were the Jews. Early on in his term of office he caused a violent disturbance by using temple funds to build an aqueduct. And there is evidence that on two or three occasions he was ruthless in suppressing religious violence. But one can sympathize with him. Religious bitterness is very difficult to deal with. The nearest modern parallel I can draw is this: imagine a fastidiously agnostic Oxford don sent to govern Northern Ireland, seething with religious tension. Can we imagine his frustration and disdain and final cynicism as he picks his way through confrontations with the IRA and UDA? No, Pontius Pilate had a difficult job to do, and it is something to his credit that he stuck it for ten years.

Towards the end of his stay in Judea he gave permission for the execution of Jesus of Nazareth. It happened about AD 33. In Matthew's Gospel Pontius Pilate and his wife were both impressed by Jesus and he did try to release him. But by this time he was a cynical and probably very tired man. So, we read, he handed over Jesus to be crucified. It happened about AD 33. He suffered under Pontius Pilate.

We do not know what happened to Pontius Pilate after that. He steps out of history, though legends abound. One has it that he later became

a Christian, and the Abyssinian Church has canonized him. Another legend has it that, like Judas,
he later committed suicide. There are legends about
his wife too. The Greek Church canonized her. We
cannot be certain of these things. All we know for
certain is that during his term of office as Governor
of Judea he crucified Jesus. And his name has been
a date-stamp on the Christian creed ever since.

But there is another reason why Pontius Pilate is
in the creed and this reason is more important and
more complex. To explain it I want to digress for
a moment. Most of us have been brought up on the
good guys versus the bad guys theory of history.
In fact, history and human nature are much more
complicated than that. I want to give an example
from politics to illustrate this. My example is about
Churchill. Some years ago I saw the controversial
play by the German playwright, Hochhuth, called
The Soldiers. In this play Hochhuth tried to prove
that Churchill was a war criminal. Apart alto-
gether from that, the play raised a fascinating and
insoluble human dilemma. Churchill went to war
to defeat the hideous spectre of Hitler's Germany.
It was Hitler's invasion of Poland that brought
Britain into the war. Towards the end of the war
things are still in the balance and Churchill is in
an appalling dilemma. He cannot beat Germany
without Russia's help, and he suspects that Stalin's
Russia is as great an evil as Hitler's Germany. In
order to make certain that Russia will not make
an independent arrangement with Germany, he

has to turn a blind eye to Russia's occupation of the East European countries, including Poland. It is expedient that Poland be sacrificed to Russia rather than have the whole of Europe perish. Here we see the anguish of the person in power. What he did was wrong. He sacrificed Poland and Eastern Europe to communist domination in order to save the rest of Europe from a Hitler–Stalin pact. What would we have done in his place?

Here we face an appalling human dilemma. Human affairs rarely allow for a simple choice between good and evil, light and darkness. Whatever we choose to do is wrong because our nature is wrong; there is a profound distortion at the root of things which makes all our choices corrupt to some degree. And this was Pilate's dilemma. He was in an appalling situation. If he released Jesus he would provoke a riot, many would be killed and reports would be sent to Rome. His own usefulness in a tense situation would be compromised. On the other hand, Jesus is innocent, and he knows it, and the whole genius of Roman law was, in theory, for the protection of human rights. How was he to act? Jesus, we read, recognized his dilemma and had compassion on him, compassion because he was in a position of power. 'Thou couldest have no power at all against me, except it were given thee from above: therefore he that delivered me unto thee hath the greater sin.' (AV) The Christian by this word is called upon to feel compassion for those in power; to sympathize with them in their dilemma.

Pilate made the inevitable decision; the only decision he could make. He sacrificed one innocent man for the sake of maintaining peace. Churchill and Poland. Pilate and Christ. What other decision was humanly possible? We would have done the same. And yet, we know both decisions were wrong. Wrong, yet unavoidable; wrong, yet inevitable. What is this tragic flaw in humanity that forces us to these decisions? And we have all made decisions like this. We have turned our backs on the needs of others, on the demands they make on us, because we have other responsibilities. We have families, we have jobs, we have unavoidable obligations. We do have these obligations, and we cannot run away from them. We live in the midst of excruciating dilemmas. *I* am Pontius Pilate. Every day I make the unavoidable decision to hand over Christ. He suffered under Pontius Pilate. I am Pontius Pilate, and he allows himself to suffer at my hands. These are some of the most momentous words in history. God loves us and pities our dilemmas. God has compassion upon our impossible predicaments. God stretches out towards us just as we are: soiled with compromises, heavy with the burden of wrong decisions, laden with greater and lesser infidelities. I am Pontius Pilate, and Christ allows himself to suffer under me. He does not hold back till I make the right decisions, till I purify myself. He comes to me, recognizing my unavoidable sinfulness and accepts me in spite of it. And the cross is the demonstration of this incredible love. God in Christ does not judge us and condemn us in our dilemmas. He himself becomes the victim of our dilemmas. He bears them in his own body on the tree.

He suffered under Pontius Pilate. I am Pontius Pilate. *I* am in the creed, because my Lord allows himself to suffer at my hands. He knows my dilemmas and my weaknesses and he takes them upon himself. And as I lay the cross upon his back he gazes at me, with compassion. Because, you see, I am Pontius Pilate.

7 * The Executioner

And when they came to a place called Golgotha
(which means the place of a skull), they offered
him wine to drink, mingled with gall; but when
he tasted it, he would not drink it. And when they
had crucified him, they divided his garments among
them by casting lots; then they sat down and kept
watch over him there.

(Matt. 27.33–36, RSV)

Caiaphas and Pontius Pilate were responsible for
the death of Jesus, but they didn't, of course, do the
dirty work themselves. The Caiaphases and Pilates
of this world never do. They may be the people
that declare the wars, but they are never the ones
that do the fighting or the dying. There are always
others, plenty of others, to do the dirty work for
them. It is always someone else who hammers in
the nails or pushes in the bayonet; it is always the
person under orders.

We don't know anything about the executioners
who laid Jesus on the cross and stretched out his
arms and prised open his fingers, before they drove
the thick nails though the thin flesh onto the beam
behind. They had nothing against him, of course,
and probably had never even heard of him. But
they would not, in any case, look him in the eyes.
Their job concentrated on his hands and his feet.
They had to forget the faces to get through the
job at all. 'Never look them in the face', the older
executioners would tell the younger, 'or you'll

never get the job done.' *His* eyes were certainly to be avoided. His eyes were great and dark with love, and to get on with the job at all they had to ignore them, turn away from them, put on a gruffness and a toughness they didn't feel. Usually the victims cursed and swore and fought like tigers, and it took several men to hold them down. This one was different. They sensed, not fear or hatred, but a terrible sorrow in him, an ancient longing which made everything seem strangely muffled and distant. It was as though this thing which was happening, this thing they were doing with that rough hammer and those cruel nails was happening somewhere else. Sure enough, it was happening here and now on this Friday morning, but it seemed to be happening somewhere else too, somewhere beyond time. It was the strangest thing. It was as if a great door shut suddenly somewhere, back beyond time, and a cry pierced them, as if God wept. And then they heard him praying: 'Father forgive them for they know not what they do.' Then they all grabbed the cross and lifted it into its socket up there on the hill, and that door shut again, and again that cry was heard somewhere else out of time. Hastily they picked up their tools and walked away, and they could not bear to turn round and look at him till they were far enough away not to see his eyes. It took two skins of wine before they could stop shivering.

History is full of them, but we know none of their names. They are the ones under orders, the ones doing a job, a filthy job, a job they must do to keep their families fed, to pay the rent. They are the ones who build the gallows and make them strong. Others send the victims. They are the ones who make sure the train to the concentration camp leaves on time. Others send the passengers. They are the ones who service the gas ovens. Others sign the papers that send in the women and children. They have a job to do, and they do it. But they never look at the faces. They have a job to do, and because they do it, because they obey orders without fuss, every tyranny in history has been built on their compliance, their reliance on wages.

But we dare not condemn them because we, too, are the executioners. We are all enclosed in this web of guilt in great ways and small. I depend for my material need upon men who live underground to dig my coal. I put my garbage on the sidewalk and someone else must lift it, tons of it, to keep my street tidy. It is in my name that young soldiers with guns are parading the streets of Northern Ireland. My fondness for tea and coffee means back-breaking labour and low wages for thousands of peasants. We are all part of one another, and somewhere another person's pain is caused by my pleasure. Mine are the hands that wield the mallet that bangs in the nails, not another's. And there is no way out of this web, this maze of guilt and responsibility for each other. It is an inescapable part of being human. We exploit and degrade one another in ways we do not even know. We are all part of one another, and we are all, in some sense, guilty of each other's miseries. There is no way we can creep out from under this guilt, once we recognize it. We cannot jump out of our own skin, nor can we purge our own guilt, no matter how hard we try.

This is why the cross of Jesus is for us both an object of sorrow and of joy. Sorrow, because this is what we do day after day. Joy, because at the very moment we bang in the nails he forgives us. No matter how hard we try, we cannot kill God's love for us. God forgives and forgives and forgives. And there is no more terrible word in any language than that, once we feel its meaning and its cost. There is no weapon effective against that unwearying love. There is nothing we can do against it. That is why one day, after all our striving and folly and flight, we will go to God, defeated, conquered by the strange victim we thought we had done with. Christ's cross will have the victory. His love will win. He knew it. It cost him dear, but he knew it. That is why he said: 'I, when I am lifted up from the earth, will draw all men to myself.'

PART 2

THE WORDS

8 * The First Word

And when they came to the place which is called
The Skull, there they crucified him, and the criminals,
one on the right and one on the left. And Jesus
said, 'Father, forgive them; for they know not what
they do'.

(Luke 23.33, RSV)

According to the evangelists Matthew, Mark,
Luke, and John, our Lord uttered seven sayings,
seven 'words', on the cross during the six hours
he hung there from nine in the morning till three
in the afternoon. The traditional arrangement is
that he uttered the first three words between the
hours of nine in the morning and noon; that he
uttered the fourth word, the central most terrible word at noon, when darkness covered the
face of the earth; and the three last words were
spoken just before three o'clock, as he yielded up
his spirit.

Luke and John each record three words, and the
fourth and central saying is contained in Matthew
and in Mark. There's nothing strange about this
apparently arbitrary distribution of sayings between
the four evangelists, because we know that most of
the traditions about our Lord were picked up and
put down by the evangelists as they had occasion,
and we know that there were various groups of
listeners on the sacred mount where they crucified him. We know that the apostles forsook

him, but we are also told that Peter followed afar off later on. He must have been lurking somewhere in the background, in the outer ring of scoffing bystanders. Mark tells us, 'And they led Jesus to the high priest; and all the chief priests and the elders and the scribes were assembled. And Peter had followed him at a distance ...' (Mark 14.53–54).

We can be quite certain that Peter wasn't the only one of the disciples who had deserted him after the arrest, who followed at a distance. Some had the courage to come more closely. We know that our Lady and the beloved apostle John were at the foot of the cross. We know that there were other women there, too. When we come to the third word, we shall note that there were several women clustered around the foot of the cross.

Incidentally, it is worth meditating on the role of women in the Passion of our Lord. Unlike the men around him, they showed courage and devotion, a courage and devotion which has frequently characterized Christian women, very often in the face of the cowardice of Christian men. The women who followed our Lord never seem to have failed him. They followed him to the end, when their more aggressive brothers had deserted him.

We must think, therefore, of various groups of bystanders around the cross, some a little on one side, some a little on the other; and we must think of our Lord raised only about eighteen inches above the bystanders. We tend to have an exalted view, a kind of Metro – Goldwyn – Mayer view, of the crucifixion. Maybe we see it in a rosy light, our Lord beautifully made-up, on an exquisitely carved crucifix, high above Calvary, like a rood screen high above a cathedral altar. This was not the case. The crucified was probably only about eighteen inches above the people who were standing around the foot of the cross, so they could very easily hear what he said.

But before we meditate on the first word, let us run over the events which preceded it.

We know our Lord was arrested in the Garden of Gethsemane in the middle of the night. We know that he went through six trials in the hours that followed, before he was finally led out to the place of execution. We know that before he bore the cross, he was scourged. Scourging was itself almost a form of capital punishment. It was hideously effective. The victim was ringed to a pillar and stripped. His back was flayed with a whip which was laced with pieces of bone or steel or iron which literally laid the man's back open. Our Lord endured all this, then he was given the cross beam and made to walk to the mount of Calvary.

When they arrived on the hill the victims were stripped naked and thrown down on the rude beams. At this point there was usually an enormous struggle. The victims would curse and swear and fight with their executioners. The contrast between the behaviour of the criminals and our Lord was both poignant and bitter. Luke tells us that as they nailed our Lord to the cross he said, 'Father, forgive them for they know not what they do.'

Forgive whom? The Romans certainly, the soldiers and the impersonal executioners, as well as Pilate, with his busy, officious desire to keep the peace in that turbulent city. And the Jews as well, who had called for his death and delivered him to Pilate to be crucified. But behind the Romans and Jews there presses the whole of mankind. Just as the city where they crucified our Lord is every city, so are his executioners all of us. The first word, then, is a word of forgiveness, and it is spoken to us who take part, in many different ways, in the crucifixions of our Lord. Part of our sin is a kind of ignorance. We know not, most of the time, what we do. Paul, in the first letter to the Corinthians, said, 'None of the rulers of this world understood, for if they had they would not have crucified the Lord of Glory.' They did not know who he was. In the great parable of judgement in Matthew, chapter 25, those who are standing before our Lord all plead ignorance: 'When did we see thee naked or hungry or thirsty or in prison?' And he answers, 'Inasmuch as ye did not do it unto the least of these my brethren, ye did not do it unto me.' We did not know that God was in all the challenges that come before us and our compassion. We did not know who was hurt by our sins. So, in a sense, we sin against ourselves ignorantly.

Do you remember our Lord's lament over the city of Jerusalem when he saw it as he was coming into it for the last time? He stopped there and gazed down upon it from the brow of the hill, and he looked at it, shining, white in the heat: 'Jerusalem, Jerusalem'. And he wept over it, we are told, because it did not know the things that belonged unto its peace. If only it had known he was sent to it! If only it had known that he wanted to gather all Jerusalem and its citizens in his arms as a hen gathers its chickens, and they would not! So we feel all the pain and patience and pity of God for us and for the ignorant ways we have denied his approach to us; all the ways we have ignorantly put him away from us.

Yet, in some sense, we *do* know what we do. Certainly, in some profound sense we do not know what we do, but in another sense we do know, because there is often a wilfulness about our sinning, about our selfishness. We know what we do, all too often. We deliberately, perversely sabotage our own joy. And we have done it so often. We have done things we know will cause us, afterwards, to burn with remorse. So, as we meditate upon this word we must think of our ignorant sins *and* our wilful sins, our crying sins and our secret sins.

All this we must meditate upon, because this scene at the very beginning of the last act of our Lord's life imposes a most intolerable truth upon us. Forgiveness is intolerable! He forgives us. He gives back to us all the pain and despite we have done to him. He is bruised and butchered by our sins, and he forgives us. This really is the heart of the Christian gospel, and it is intolerable because most of us do not want to be forgiven. We want somehow to make up for it, we want to earn it; or we want to be punished for it. We want to feel a smouldering, gnawing kind of guilt, but he will not permit it. He forgives us. He suffers what we do, that we might amend freely. How can we carry on one moment longer in iniquity when we see what it does to him and how he bears it?

This is the heart of the Christian gospel. The cross is an advertisement, showing us the consequences to God of our activities. What we see in the cross of our Lord Jesus Christ is an eternal truth, as it were, revealed, advertised before us, showing what are the consequences of our actions, and the intolerable response of God, which is forgiveness: 'Father, forgive them.'

There can only be two responses to that intolerable word of forgiveness. The first is to accept the forgiveness. Identify in you what hammers in the nails. Do not shirk that act of self-examination. Know the worst against yourself, and then receive the forgiveness that is freely offered. But, as you gaze upon that advertisement of the eternal pain, passion, and forgiveness of God, purpose amendment, for how can you bear to let it go on one moment longer? That forgiving pain of God

48

must have an end sometime. Purpose amendment, so that henceforth you will not be the one who drives the nails into our Lord, but one who, with him, heals the pain and shares the burden.

9 * The Second Word

One of the criminals who were hanged railed at him, saying, 'Are you not the Christ? Save yourself and us!' But the other rebuked him, saying, 'Do you not fear God, since you are under the same sentence of condemnation? And we indeed justly; for we are receiving the due reward of our deeds; but this man has done nothing wrong.' And he said, 'Jesus, remember me when you come in your kingly power.' And he said to him, 'Truly, I say to you, today you will be with me in Paradise.'

(Luke 23.39–43, RSV)

The two criminals heard and saw everything that happened to our Lord on the Mount of Calvary, and one of them joined in the mockery. It is a fact that victims often co-operate with their persecutors in crimes against other victims. It is one of the strangest elements of human perversity, that there are always some among the weak who will join with the strong in oppressing the weak. There are always some victims who will join the bullies in victimizing others. All those who in history and in daily life join their oppressors debase themselves in the face of their own tormentors. Is there a grosser, more demeaning spectacle in history than the sight of this coarse and brutal criminal in his own death throes, turning his head to join with the rabble, who have put him

up where he is, in taunting his fellow victim? The weak who join the bully in persecution: have we done it, perhaps? Persecution by the persecuted? Have we, in order to
avoid drawing attention to our own weakness,
joined with the strong in pursuing other weak
people?

The weak turn against themselves. They are
miracles of perversity. But there is another miracle at that moment on the hill where they crucified
him: the miracle of awareness. Maybe the penitent thief had heard Jesus during the two or
three years of his ministry. Maybe he knew
someone who had been healed by him. Maybe
his sister or his brother had followed Jesus and
had seen the mighty works that he did, and
had heard the searching words that he spoke
and had seen his tenderness and his care for the
weak. We do not know. Certainly, it would
have been difficult not to have heard something
about Jesus. Maybe this thief had been mildly
intrigued by our Lord. But he was tough. It is
a strange thing, this toughness, isn't it, which
is really a kind of weakness? I know a little bit about this because I went to a tough
school and was a tough kid. Yet, God called
me to be a priest, and I was acutely embarrassed! I remember how I was unable to tell
my friends I was going to be a priest. It was
a weak kind of thing to be. I was embarrassed.
And this kind of weakness, which vests itself

in a swaggering, macho kind of toughness, is really evidence of a feeble inner life, or no inner life at all.

Maybe the penitent thief was like this. He was a man's man, who never really thought below the surface of life until at this moment he was brought to a moment of truth. There are two elements in this moment of truth and realization. The first is obviously his own death. The thought of one's own death, as Dr Johnson reminded us, marvellously concentrates the mind. All temporal and transitory considerations were cut away. There was nothing left for him among those with whom he used to run. The world held nothing, and he gazed into his own death, and death was the prelude to revelation. It still is. It cuts through the chatter and noise and distraction of our mind, and makes us mind the things that matter. 'Memento Mori', the ancients used to say, 'Remember to die, remember you are this day on the way to death.' And what is it that matters to you at that point? We must all of us find these moments to concentrate on the certainty that there will one day be an end, maybe sooner than we think. The man on the cross came to that moment, that prelude to revelation which the certainty of his own death meant.

Then he did another thing: he really looked at Jesus for the first time, and he was suddenly overwhelmed. Doubtless, he had heard a bit here and there about this extraordinary man who had the whole of Jerusalem in an uproar, but he had never really himself looked at Jesus. Now, here he looks and looks hard, and everything else is blotted out as he sees the majesty, the humility, and the strength of the man. The eyes of Christ hold him. He looks at Christ, and he has a moment of revelation. At last he recognizes the truth. We must do the same. If we would find Jesus, we must look steadily at him. We spend so much time looking at other faces, our minds hurtling distractedly in every direction. If we would know and be freed by the truth, we must learn to look at Jesus, maybe for the first time. We do not give ourselves a chance otherwise. Look to Jesus, fix your eyes upon him. The criminal did, and then he made his clumsy, uneducated act of faith. His mind was a jumble of messianic notions, political revolution, and spiritual longings. He turns to the majestic, yet wounded figure beside him and says, 'When you come into your kingdom, remember me.' And the response of Jesus is momentous and comforting. 'Verily I say unto thee, this day thou shalt be with me in paradise.'

The word 'paradise' comes from the Persian, as a loan word to the Greek, meaning an enclosed park or pleasure garden. The orginal Greek translation of the Old Testament used it for the Garden of Eden, and then it was developed as a superterrestrial place of blessedness, a paradise, the place where God was. The word is only used twice elsewhere in the New Testament. In 2 Corinthians, Paul describes one of his own mystical experiences: 'And I know that this man was caught up into Paradise — whether in the body or out of the body I do not know, God knows.' (2 Cor. 12.3, RSV)

Paul was caught up out of the body and given a glimpse of heaven. And we find the words again in the Book of Revelation: 'He who has an ear, let him hear what the Spirit says to the churches. To him who conquers I will grant to eat of the tree of life, which is in the paradise of God.' (Rev. 2.7, RSV)

Our Lord assured the penitent that that very day he would be with him after death with God in heaven. It is pointless to speculate or try to be specific about the precise order or levels of God's presence, or get into theological disputes about the nature of paradise, or whether there are grades in it, or whether we really deserve to enter it. All that matters is that our Lord promised a life after death: 'Today thou shall be with me in paradise.' It is important to understand the depth and scope of this promise, because our Lord knew of what he spoke. He came from the Father, 'He came down from heaven', as our creed says, and he assured us of eternal life. This is one of the most important elements of his teaching.

Jesus said to her, 'I am the resurrection and the life; he who believes in me, though he die, yet shall he live, and whoever lives and believes in me shall never die. Do you believe this?

(John 11.25–26, RSV)

Let not your hearts be troubled; believe in God, believe also in me. In my Father's house are many rooms; if it were not so, would I have told you that I go to prepare a place for you? And when I go and prepare a place for you, I will come again and will take you to myself, that where I am you may be also. And you know the way where I am going.

(John 14.1–4, RSV)

The Christian faith is based on a conviction of the life of the world to come. Paul says, 'If only in this life we have hope, then we are of all men the most miserable and foolish.' Christ came to forgive and sanctify us. He came to teach us about the true nature of God. And he came to assure us of life after death. We are by this word to receive that promise into our hearts, and let it strengthen us for the great struggle of our Christian life. We have the whole of eternity to aspire to, to long for. With that knowledge, we are not separated from those we love. We are not bereft, but following after those 'we have loved long since and lost a while', in Newman's great phrase. And we are not bereft even of those we have never known in the flesh. Have you never felt close to the great heroes and saints as you have read their words and meditated upon their lives? We are not separated from them. I have often felt them beside me.

Nothing can ultimately separate us from the love of God, and those who are separated from us by death. So this word asks us to do two things. It asks us to look at Jesus, maybe for the first time: look away from all else: look only unto him. And then it asks us to look through Jesus into eternity, to the great homeland that awaits us, the land of the Trinity, deep heaven, a place prepared for us by our blessed Lord. So look to Jesus, and look through Jesus, to the life that is promised to us, which will know no end.

10 * *The Third Word*

> When the soldiers had crucified Jesus they took his garments and made four parts, one for each soldier ... But the tunic was without seam, woven from top to bottom; so they said to one another, 'Let us not tear it, but cast lots for it to see whose it shall be.' ... So the soldiers did this; but standing by the cross of Jesus were his mother, and his mother's sister, Mary the wife of Clopas, and Mary Magdalene. When Jesus saw his mother, and the disciple whom he loved standing near, he said to his mother, 'Woman, behold your son!' Then he said to the disciple, 'Behold your mother!' And from that hour the disciple took her to his own home.
>
> (John 19.23–27, RSV)

Almost certainly these women standing near the cross were the ones who had provided the garments which the soldiers greedily and callously divided among themselves.

> And the twelve were with him, and also some women who had been healed of evil spirits and infirmities: Mary, called Magdalene, from whom seven demons had gone out, and Joanna, the wife of Chuza, Herod's steward, and Susanna, and many others, who provided for them out of their means.
>
> (Luke 8.1–3, RSV)

These women provided for our Lord and his band of apostles. It is conceivable that they had made the very garments that were

57

being divided among themselves by the soldiers.

The women watched the four grizzled and unaffected soldiers pulling off his clothes and dividing them up. One grabs the seamless robe or the tunic. After an argument they decide to gamble for it. The tunic they gambled for was the undergarment which was worn next to the skin. As the soldiers were wrestling and gambling over what was obviously a fine garment, was the woman who had made it standing there, thinking of the love that she had poured into it? The Gospels do not attempt more than a spare description of the scene but we can enter imaginatively into it. Those women loved this man as no man had ever been loved. One had borne him in her womb and suckled him at her breast. Of course, she had been warned that a sword would pierce her own heart, but there was no way of preparing for the sight of her own son being beaten through the streets of Jerusalem and then stripped naked on a cross. Apart from our Lady, two of the women were almost certainly particularly close to Jesus. The mother of 'the disciple whom Jesus loved', the one who had grasped most truly the real spirit and meaning of his work, must have felt a special bond to Jesus. Then there was Mary Magdalene whom he had healed, to whom he had given a purpose and a meaning, and whose devotion to him was total and extravagantly great. Mary Magdalene comes out of the gospel narrative shining. She it is who is there at the garden tomb where they laid him, to whom our Lord speaks on the first Easter Day. And we know that John was standing by, the only apostle whose courage equalled that of the women.

While this little scene is being acted out, our Lord looks down upon his mother and the little group at the foot of the cross. He is going into his last battle now; the time is approaching for his final struggle. So far his thoughts on the cross have only been for others, his enemies, his executioners: 'Father, forgive them'; for the penitent thief: 'Today thou shalt be with me in paradise.' Before he entered into the deep inner struggle that awaited him he performed one last act of human concern as he went into that dark and terrible struggle which we shall try to uncover when we meditate on the fourth word. As he girds himself for that final and awful moment, he looks down and sees his blessed mother and the beloved disciple, and he delivers her into his keeping: 'Woman, behold thy son. Son, behold thy mother.' And we read that he took her to his own home from that very hour. William Temple suggests that Jesus wanted John to take our Lady away at that very moment, so she would be spared the last awful struggle of his dying. We cannot be certain of this, but we know that John was there at the very end. Perhaps he took her to his home in Jerusalem and then hurried back to Calvary for the end.

It is strange that he handed his mother over in this way to John, because there was a group in the

Gospels called 'the brethren of our Lord'. Maybe they were the sons of Joseph by a previous marriage. The fact that Jesus delivered Mary into the care of John is evidence that Jesus was her only son. John was the son of our Lady's sister, Mary's closest blood relative. Our Lord, in his last act, gave his mother into his cousin's keeping. It was an act of filial piety; an act of concern, of love; the final putting of his own human affairs in order before his final journey.

One tradition tells us that our Lady stayed with John in Jerusalem and died aged fifty-nine. Another tradition tells us that he took her to Ephesus with him. There is absolute certainty that John lived until a great age in Ephesus. Certainly, we know that our Lady was taken from that very hour into the keeping of the beloved apostle.

But the act was more than an act of simple provision for the welfare of his mother. In a deeper sense it was the creating of a new family; it was the beginning of the Church. Our Lady, in one sense, was the mother of the Church, which is itself a mother. Our Lord's last words to the world set up a new type of family, in which not blood, but charity would be the law that binds. So we must, when we meditate upon this third word of our Lord on the cross, think not only of his filial piety, of his love for his mother, but think also of the Church which is our mother. And since we are the Church, we are to be in some mysterious sense, mothers to others. We are to care in tenderness for those who are alongside us. The Church is to become a new kind of family, a new kind of fellowship. 'Behold thy son, behold thy mother.'

11 * *The Fourth Word*

And when the sixth hour had come, there was darkness over the whole land until the ninth hour. And at the ninth hour Jesus cried with a loud voice, 'Eloi, eloi, lama sabachthani?', which means, 'My God, my God, why hast thou forsaken me?'

(Mark 15.33–34, RSV)

Now we come to the fourth and central word, recorded by Mark and Matthew, and I want to try to enter into its meaning by describing four events.

I remember visiting a parishioner in Edinburgh who never forgot the Friday of a particular Trades Fortnight. She was married, with two children under twelve years old, and they had been looking forward to going on holiday. She expected her husband home some time in the middle of the afternoon on that first Friday of the Trades Fortnight, but he never turned up; he did not come back. She waited for days. She could not go to his work, because it was closed for two weeks, but she did make enquiries and she discovered that on the Friday when the works closed he had taken his holiday pay, every penny that was owed to him, and what was being saved for his retirement, and he had gone off to the south of England with another woman. He had not warned her. He had not informed anyone. She pieced the story together many months later after she had put a private detective on to it. And she was torn in two by the information; she felt forsaken. She had no inkling that this was going to happen, that he could have carefully and coldly planned to walk out like this. There had been no forewarning, no preparation. She felt utterly forsaken.

And the second story is about a friend of mine who worked in a mental hospital. There was a little girl there who did nothing but cry. She never spoke to anyone; she simply sat and cried. Finally, a brilliant and patient therapist discovered her story. She had lived alone with her mother, and one night, in the middle of the night, her mother gave birth to a baby, whom she promptly smothered. Then she wrapped the baby in an old bed cloth and gave it to this child, who was then ten years old, and told her to take the baby to an abandoned building opposite and leave it there. The little girl obeyed, numb with horror. She was found hours later walking through the streets of the city with tears streaming down her face. The police found her, but she never spoke another word until the therapist managed to piece together the hideous reality that she had experienced. And what came out was the sense of forsakenness. This mother whom she had loved had gone into a place she did not understand. She had done hideous things and used her as an accomplice, so she felt forsaken by all she had ever loved.

And I think of a young married couple who were very much in love. He phoned up in the afternoon of their anniversary and said, 'I am taking you out to dinner tonight – get ready.' But he never arrived home. Instead, a policeman arrived and said he had been killed on the way home in a hit and run accident. And she felt forsaken. She felt utterly crushed and numb.

Finally, let me give an experience of my own, less dramatic perhaps, but painful to me. When I had been a priest for five years, I realized that I no longer believed in God. I felt forsaken. Forsaken, even though I felt there was no God to forsake me, and for eighteen months I had to go through the motions of my faith, my priesthood, with no sense of the presence or reality of God.

These are patterns of forsakenness. To be forsaken is to be cut off from what gives our life meaning and beauty, what holds our life together, what makes us continue. And we come, in the fourth word, the most mysterious of the words, to an experience of forsakenness that nothing we have ever experienced can parallel, because it is a unique level of dereliction. Nevertheless, some of the ways in which we have experienced the depths will give us a tiny clue, a tiny analogy, to the reality of what was going on up there on the cross at noon on that Friday. Our Lord defined himself by his closeness to God. He spoke of his *Father*. Often, he went apart and prayed to the Father. Always, he lived as in the sight of his Father. 'He that has seen me has seen the Father', 'I and the Father are one', he said. There was a union between him and the

Father which was total. They pulsed together. Our creed describes it as a total identity, 'being of one substance'. And this communion with the Father, this being what the Father was, had given him the courage to endure everything that the world threw at him. It had sustained him against every temptation to disobey his Father's will. Here he is now, forsaken by all in the world, forsaken, even by his disciples. Only a few women and his beloved John were there, but he could not reach them. He was only a few feet away, yet an infinity of distance separated him from them. And maybe by this time his mother had been taken away by John, as the great battle overwhelmed him. He was forsaken by all he had loved on earth, but sustained still by his Father. And, suddenly, the ground of his inner security disappears. God withdraws. The only thing that had kept Jesus together is taken away completely. He is forsaken. Suddenly, he feels absolutely bereft, even of God. The tense of the verb is very specific, it's an aorist, which is punctiliar in sense. It had happened in a moment. 'My God, my God, why hast thou forsaken me?' He was not describing a general condition, but a moment, like a stab or a thunderbolt. Nothing now sustains him. God goes forth from himself, un-Gods himself. We cannot enter into the heart of this word, this paradox, but maybe we can enter a few inches of the experience. God submitted himself to a forsakenness, a desertion of his own nature, for our sakes. This is the only time in the New Testament that Jesus personally addresses God as 'God'. Not, this time, '*Abba*', Daddy, Father, but *God*: 'My God, my God, why hast thou forsaken me?'

How can we possibly enter this experience? Most of us experience forsakenness as something external to ourselves, however close the person who has forsaken us may have been. Is schizophrenia, perhaps, in some of its forms, an anology? Something within your mind splits you apart. The experience of those who are going mad must approach this sense of absolute dereliction, a sense of being torn away from your own self. But we cannot really enter into this experience by our minds alone. The poets help us best.

> O the mind, mind has mountains; cliffs of
>   fall
> Frightful, sheer, no-man-fathomed. Hold
>   them cheap
> May who ne'er hung there. Nor does long
>   our small
> Durance deal with that steep or deep.
>   (Gerard Manley Hopkins)

That was the experience of a man, but it may help us to approach the reality of that unique moment on the cross when God forsook his own Son. At any rate, here we are in the very heart of the Christian faith, and it is a mystery, dazzling in its blackness. There are elements in it that we can, at least, apply our minds to.

Our Lord was identified totally with our experience. We know that one of the meanings of his life was a recapitulation of the whole human experience. He recapitulated everything that had happened to humanity. Every level of abandonment he plumbed. He united himself to it all, to every desolate experience, every forsaken child. He identified with it all. He went down into the depths. Certain strands of the New Testament say that at this moment he went into Hell and harrowed it. Paul, in the letter to the Ephesians, talks about the one who 'ascended' and 'also descended into the innermost parts of the earth'. These are the phrases that come in flashes of vision, of insight and revelation. What they seem to mean is that our Lord went to the very bottom of the bottom of history, and became identified with it, uniting himself to it, and by so doing, somehow, redeemed it. By bearing it, he transformed it, because in some sense the tragedy of human history is caused by our flight from responsibility. There is a sense in which we are ignorant; we do not know what we do. But there is another sense in which we have made our own misery, and yet are impotent to help ourselves. Somehow we are brought to a judgement which we cannot bear, and he himself bears it in his own body on the tree. Now we know that it cannot overwhelm us forever. That is why we meditate upon the cross, although, if we had seen it in its awful reality we must surely have shielded our eyes. This is the epicentre, the total eclipse, the murder of God, which gave us life in a sense beyond defining. By the bearing of all sorrow, Christ saved the world. But no words can possibly explain the reality of that moment and its meaning. What we must do is to try to clutch the edges of this utter forsakenness. It will deepen our pity and compassion for others, but it will also afford us a moment of identity with the Son of God, who was forsaken by God in order to restore us to that place in God's heart, which we, in our ignorant wilfulness, had ourselves forsaken.

12 * *The Fifth Word*

> After this Jesus, knowing that all was now finished,
> said (to fulfil the scripture), 'I thirst.'
>
> (John 19.28, RSV)

It is very near the end now. The period of absolute
dereliction, of forsakenness, which we thought
about in the fourth word, that central moment
of the drama, cannot be measured in time. Maybe
he was in despair, in that forsaken place, for two
or three hours. We do know that he plumbed the
very depths of Hell, the lowest parts of the earth.
As Paul says in Ephesians, 'In saying he ascended,
what does it mean but that he also descended into
the lower parts of the earth?' He went right down
into the very bottom of the human experience of
misery. And if we had been there, what would
we have seen? Nothing. There is a great silence
around the cross. Not a word is spoken after this
word, until the very end. But there was no lack of
activity. Indeed, it was at this time that the most
intense activity was taking place, because this was
when Jesus was confronting fully and finally the
reality that tyrannized God's creation. This final
confrontation can only be put in the language of
struggle, of mystical conflict. This is what the old
hymn writers did: 'Sing, my tongue, the glorious
battle, sing the ending of the fray.' This was the
final battle. The old writers loved that kind of

warlike language. 'The royal banners forward go, the Cross shines forth in mystic glow.' But it was a strange battle. Doubtless his body was moving and twitching in the final agonies of death. One of the most hideous things about crucifixion was the constant battle for air. The poor victims had to push themselves up on their feet in order to get air into their lungs, and then they would slump down again in excruciating pain. The victim was, therefore, constantly battling for breath.

But the real battle, the glorious battle of which we sing, and for which 'the royal banners forward go', was fought in silence and blackness, in some deep place we can only visit in our minds. There was noise all around, but there was silence there. Then he emerges through it, and he gathers his strength for the final act of obedience, the final act of triumphant surrender. The last words on the cross are words of triumph, although they are poignant. As he comes out of this great, black pit, this forsaken place, this howling wilderness where he has been, he needs to refresh himself for his final act of strength. He is going now to drink the cup that at Gethsemane he prayed might pass from him. But he has fought the fight, he has kept the faith, he will now be faithful to the end.

There was a tradition, a merciful practice, that the victims of crucifixion were drugged. It was one of the social works, one of the acts of mercy of the wealthy ladies of Jerusalem. They would bring to the scene of crucifixion bowls of drugged wine in order to anaesthetize the poor victims who were dying hideous deaths. As we know, our Lord had refused the cup of drugged wine. He had refused it, presumably, because he wanted a clear head for battle. He did not want to be in a stupor. But now that the battle is almost over, he wishes to be able to speak, and he cannot. His throat is parched. It must have been heartbreaking for those who loved him, seeing his mouth moving and his tongue dry and protruding, as they remembered how he had spoken, 'because no man ever spoke the way this man spoke', we are told. Words that comforted, words that scorched, kind words, words of depth and beauty, no man spoke like this man. Now he can scarcely speak at all, yet he manages to croak, 'I thirst.' It was the only thing approaching a complaint that he said on the cross, and it was no complaint. He was about to take a practical step, because he wanted to prepare himself for his last words. How could he declare the glory that had been won if he could not speak? He wants to be able to speak, and the kindly soldiers (and one must remember this act, as well as their indifferent brutality) had with them a flask of cheap sour wine called by the Gospel writers, 'vinegar'. It was the common soldiers' drink. They were probably drinking it as the afternoon wore on. One of them tips a little of it onto the end of a sponge (there was no way of holding a cup to the lips of a crucified man) and puts it on the end of a cane, a branch of hyssop. His mouth was probably within reach of an average man's arm, up there, about eighteen inches above the ground. Jesus sucks a little of the sour wine.

But there is more to the act than the straightforward physical discomfort of thirst. Nothing in John's Gospel is simple. John always wants us to understand two or three things at the same time, and one of the things we must remember here, indeed ought to remember throughout our reading of the crucifixion narrative, is the prevailing background of the Old Testament. The central word of the cross is the first verse of Psalm 22: 'My God, my God, why hast thou forsaken me? Why art thou so far from helping me, from the words of my groaning?' To the first Christians that psalm irresistibly asserted itself as they meditated on the Passion. They also heard Psalm 69: 'They gave me poison for food, and for my thirst they gave me vinegar to drink.' We know that our Lord himself was almost certainly meditating on the scriptures as he hung there. He knew them so well. He taught us how to use them, how to make them part of our very being, and this cry of his, 'I thirst', echoes much in the Psalter. 'As a hart longs for flowing streams, so longs my soul for thee, O God.' 'My soul thirsts for God, for the living God. When shall I come and behold the face of God?' 'My tears have been my food day and night, while men continually say to me night and day, where is your God?' 'My soul thirsts for God.' And there was Psalm 63: 'O God, thou art my God, I seek thee, my soul thirsts for thee; my flesh faints for thee, as in a dry and weary land where no water is.' That is where our Lord had just been – in a dry and weary land where no water was, and he emerged from that dark wilderness with a thirst for God.

So, first of all, we must understand our Lord's real physical thirst and his need to slake his throat, so that he might proclaim the great words that were to end the drama of the cross. There is a deeper meaning to the verse, as well, because he emerged from the period of desolation with an enormous longing for God, a homesickness for the Father, a heart-hunger. Have you never felt it? Have you never felt an enormous longing for God? You may not ever have really known him, you may doubt his very existence, yet your heart hungers. 'My soul thirsts for God, yea even for the living God.' It comes to you sometimes in a dark church, in the quietness of dawn. It can come in the moorland. It can come when you see the first daffodils of spring. It can come in many ways: a sudden clutching of the heart, and a thirst for God. 'O God, thou art my God, I seek thee, my soul thirsts for thee, my flesh faints for thee.' After the great loss of God which he had experienced, our Lord experienced an overwhelming longing, the kind of longing that overwhelms us after a long separation from someone we love. 'I thirst for the living God.' Our Lord used this image of thirst many times, especially as recorded by John.

He called himself a fountain of living waters. He said, 'Come to me all who thirst. Out of me will flow streams of living water.' Jesus assuages our thirst for God, the dryness we wish to irrigate.

That is one of the meanings of this profound saying. But there is another kind of thirst. There is a thirst for the souls of men and women. There was an enormous tenderness in Jesus, though the proud and self-righteous never saw it. They only heard the words that cut like swords. But there were many others, such as the small and the despised, the children, who instinctively knew they could come to him; or the sinners who dared not lift up their eyes in the temple, and who remained in the darkest parts of the church. 'Lord, be merciful to me, a sinner', they confidently pled. The Roman soldiers, even, in their coarseness and rough honesty, our Lord always had a word for. All of these saw his grace, and felt his tenderness and strong love, and they were surprised at the effect he had on them, surprised by a sudden sense of longing for God. They would stop and catch themselves, and recognize that in this man's strong and grieving tenderness for them was something of the longing of God. What must it have been like to have looked into those strong, grieving eyes, and felt that love? No wonder that many of the poor sinners we read about in the New Testament were smitten with great emotion and were given to bouts of tears, extravagant gestures of love, like the woman who anointed his feet and wiped them dry with the hair of her head. They were quite undone by the reality of the sense of the presence of God in Christ. They were smitten by the longing for them that poured out of him. He thirsted for them and they could sense it.

Literally, then, he thirsted. He wishes to prepare himself for the final words. He also thirsted for God, figuratively. After the night, after the darkness, after the wilderness, he rediscovered a great longing, a great homesickness for the Father who had forsaken him. Finally, he thirsts for us, he longs for all of us to seek after him and find him. He thirsts for us, as we in our way thirst for him, and as we must thirst for the souls of other men and women, so that they too will know where to find the fountain of living waters.

13 * The Sixth Word

When Jesus had received the vinegar, he said, 'It is finished'; and he bowed his head and gave up his spirit.

(John 19.30, RSV)

Before I learned to think on to a typewriter, I used to write my sermons out in longhand in big notebooks. I still have them all, great big notebooks full of handwritten sermons. I no longer need to do that, but I like those volumes of old sermons. They are very disorganized, and they are not annotated. It is not possible to tell when a particular sermon was preached, unless you can discover some piece of internal evidence which allows you to date it. I like keeping those notebooks, and I shall always keep them. Although I am a great chucker-outer of things, I will never chuck those out.

As well as having those volumes of my own sermons, I also have a complete set of another man's notebooks. A friend gave them to me. Unlike mine, these notebooks are well organized. One says on it: 'Aberdeen 1928: Epiphany; Lent; Easter; October; Angels; four sermons on "the World, the Flesh and the Devil".' In this book there are about forty sermons written out, and there is even a table of contents. I have a complete set of this priest's notebooks, and some of them are very dog-eared. I don't read them, however. I hold them on my lap, sort of flick through them and pick out the odd word here and there. They are a kind of sacrament to me. I get a strange sort of physical charge out of simply looking at them. Let me try to explain what I mean. I am not an old-sermon-fetishist, nor do I nurse strange longings for old notebooks. I am fascinated, because these old sermons, over seventy years old, and some even older than that, represent another priest's struggles with the reality of Christ. I find something moving and supportive and very wistful in these notebooks, as I think of that priest in his study in Aberdeen, all those years ago, wrestling with the same angels, meditating on the same Christ, conjuring the same history that I wrestle with, conjure up and meditate upon, in 1995. I get from these books a sense of the presence of Christ. They convey to me the reality, the present, contemporary reality of Christ. He was real to this man as, in a strange way, he is real to me, as I wrestle with his illusive but over-whelming reality.

One man defined preaching as, 'a manifestation of the Incarnate Word, from the written word, by the spoken word.' The Incarnate Word, the Word of God, who became flesh two thousand years ago and walked the earth, was crucified under Pontius Pilate, and rose again from the dead, is made manifest today when the written words of the New Testament are made clear by the spoken words of the preacher. By expounding the Scripture faith-fully, the preacher makes Christ manifest. There is a chain of succession, an actualizing of the presence

77

of Christ, which comes through this strange and mysterious activity of preaching. When genuine preaching really happens, Christ is made present. There is a revelation of the Incarnate Word. So preachers have to be solitary a lot of the time. You can best meet the Incarnate Word in solitude. Christ becomes manifest in that solitude.

That is one reason why I look at this man's notebooks. I see him wrestling with the same Christ I wrestle with, and humblingly, haltingly trying to put down on paper what can never really be put into words: the reality of the universal Christ, in Jerusalem two thousand years ago, in Aberdeen sixty years ago and in Edinburgh today. Preachers, for all their dumbness and confusion, nevertheless know that Christ is the real and living one. So our Good Friday meditations are not about a poignant defeat which we simply mourn over. They are really about a strange victory which released Christ for time and for eternity. On Good Friday, we celebrate a great victory for this man who was delivered into the hands of sinners, who crucified him and put him to a terrible shame, and *was by that very action* delivered unto glory.

We have to read these events on two levels. There is, first of all, the level of history, the human level, which is the bleak, terrible story of the mocking and doing to death of the poor man of Nazareth. The worst that we know in our human nature is paraded there. It is all that, and it remains that, and yet, at the same time, it is the work of

God. There is an eternal chemistry, transmuting, transfiguring this transient horror into something that goes on forever, and concerns us today. The defeat of Christ in time was also the triumph and glorification of God on a level that transcends and encompasses time. John uses two words almost interchangeably to describe this. He talks about the crucifixion and the glorification of Christ as one and the same thing. To the beholders that death was the end, the ignominious defeat of a pretender. But to the eyes of faith it was the glorification of Christ and this paradox, this bi-dimensionality comes out perfectly in the sixth word, 'It is finished.' The word does not just mean, 'It's over, it's at an end.' It does mean that, of course, but John is always playing word games with us, because he wants us to ponder more deeply. His word *tetelestai* means it is *accomplished*, it is *fulfilled*, it is *achieved*.

The other evangelists say here that Jesus cried in a loud voice. This, according to John, is what he cried: 'It is *accomplished*. It is *finished*. The work I came to do is done.' God in Christ recapitulates humanity's history. Our tragedy is our disobedience, our resistance to reality, our pettiness. The triumph of Christ is his obedience, his grasp of reality. In Christ our whole human experience was rerun, this time properly. By his obedience, he justifies us. He reconstitutes our nature. The great word the church fathers use to describe this is 'recapitulation'. Everything was done over again in him, the representative man.

So *tetelestai,* 'it is finished', is not a sad and wistful word. It is, rather, a shout of victory. In the words of a German theologian:

> At these words you hear fetters burst, and prison walls falling down; barriers as high as heaven are overthrown, and gates which had been closed for thousands of years again move on their hinges.
> (F. W. Krummacher, 'The Risen Redeemer')

The fourth word was the moment of the assault of all that is *not* God against the will of God, and it was the moment when our Lord's most intense struggle began. But he overcame it. He burst through it by the power of his suffering, and his obedient love, and he won the victory.

Paul uses a similar expression in 2 Timothy:

> For I am already on the point of being sacrificed; the time of my departure has come. I have fought the good fight, I have finished the race, I have kept the faith. Henceforth there is laid up for me the crown of righteousness, which the Lord, the righteous judge, will award to me on that Day, and not only to me but also to all who have loved his appearing.
> (2 Timothy 4.6–8, RSV)

This is the end of the race for Christ. He bursts through the finishing tape. 'It is finished' is a word that should echo gloriously and never be muttered sorrowfully. Though it is a word, humanly speaking, of sadness and parting, it is, in fact, the ultimate word of his triumph. 'It is accomplished.'

14 * The Seventh Word

Then Jesus, crying with a loud voice, said, 'Father, into thy hands I commit my spirit!' And having said this he breathed his last.

(Luke 23.46, RSV)

We should allow a little lapse of time between the sixth and seventh words on the cross, between 'It is accomplished' and 'Into thy hands I commit my spirit.' After his triumphant claim, 'It is accomplished', Jesus bows his head, and hands over his spirit to God. The words again trap us. We normally think of this as a sort of final defeat, a last giving up and dying. We talk about struggling against death and finally giving in to it, but this is not at all the emphasis in our Lord's dying and in this account of it. The emphasis is all upon death as a *free act.* Jesus was not *killed,* he *died.* He gave up the spirit, he controlled the event. Death for Jesus was a free act. The very moment of the extinction of life was a moment he controlled. The words are important. John tells us Jesus *gave up* his spirit, he handed it over, or he dismissed it. There is the suggestion of controlled direction by Jesus of what was happening. There is no passivity in this dying. In this death the person who died was in control of the moment of death.

There is a major truth concealed in this apparently puzzling event. It is a truth which is controversial and can be expressed in different ways. According to certain thinkers, all human actions, including thought, are simply the result of a complex and predetermined mechanism. The very thoughts that we think, the mind that moves, is simply the action of the brain – there is nothing beyond the physical mechanism. That is not the Christian view, of course, but it is not even a very sensible view. It certainly does not seem to be consistent with reality. Is it not odd to have brainwaves that explain themselves to themselves? Who are they explaining to anyway? Behaviourism, physical determinism is, in fact, pervasive in its influence, and it does affect how we understand ourselves.

It is not the most ancient or the most sensible tradition, and it is certainly not the scriptural tradition. According to the Christian tradition we are not simply bodies which manage to think and explain themselves. According to our tradition we are *incarnate spirits*. We are spirits expressing themselves in bodies. A person is an embodied spirit. There is a reality which stands apart from the reality of the body, and should in fact direct and control the body. That is the theory. The fact is a little less straightforward. It is truer to say that we are spirits *learning* to control and guide the total reality of the person. Plato expressed it well in his parable of the charioteer, in which he said the horses were the appetites and the will was the charioteer. In an integrated, mature person the horses are driven in the direction of the charioteer's choosing. In a disordered and tumultuous nature, the horses plunge in different ways or they go only where they please. Plato taught from that parable that we must learn to integrate our personalities, so that our nature is moved at the behest of the governing principle of our personality which is *spirit*. In fact, we usually experience the opposite. We are usually driven by our passions and governed by our appetites. Rather than driving the chariot, we are usually driven by it.

Nevertheless, though we may be spirits who are only learning to be what we are supposed to be, this idea does correspond with our experience of the complexity of our personality. We are not simple, biological mechanisms. We are profounder and more complex than that. There is in us an experience of inwardness, an experience of transcendence of our own very natures. The very wrestling that we do with ourselves is witness to the fact. And we have seen something of it in others. We have seen in others the presence of a great strength and conviction which stands even against death itself, and the tyranny of the appetites and the passions. We see this picture of directed harmony and control at its ideal in Christ. Christ is a representative person. In Christ the physical and affective and mental natures were controlled by Spirit, though not without struggle. We have hints in the New Testament of the great struggles of Christ as he sought to recapitulate, rerun properly for the first time, the history of our human nature.

As the sixth cry testifies, he accomplished what he was sent to do. He struggled, he wrestled, but ultimately his life went where he directed it. Compare that with what we know of ourselves: think of those gusts of temper which erupt in us from some boiler-house inside our unconscious; think of those rushes of sexual passion which overwhelm us; think of the ungovernable malice and bitterness of spirit, which often swell up within us. These are some of the forms which energy assumes in us, taking over and driving us far beyond our will.

So we develop a sort of 'victim' theory of our own nature, in which the pressure of the life spirit is felt to be vague, while the physical energies are powerful. And this is the way we think about our death. We assume that even at death we shall be a little piece of thistledown or flotsam. We shall be moved by events outside us. In fact, most people today die that way. They are not in control of their own dying. Death *happens* to them. It is not anything they can do anything about.

That is not what we learn from Christ and those who have lived with something of his courage. For them life becomes something that they live, not something that simply happens to them. Death itself becomes a free, personal act. It is no longer an enemy which sneaks up on us. It is the final act of our life. According to our Lord's example, death is something we can freely choose, indeed must choose, because it corresponds to the reality of personality as free spirit. Death has been defeated and robbed of its sting, and is something we can now make our own.

This is what he did. His last word was a giving back to God of that life which had come from God. 'Father, into thy hands I return my Spirit.' His death was a free act. This was the way of Christ, the free man, probably the only really free person, the only really complete person. So his death, as well as being a great and awful tragedy, is yet a triumph of the Spirit, because it is controlled at every point, not by the human actors in the dramas, by the executioners, by Pilate, by Herod, by Annas and Caiaphas; nor even by the very action of his own body with its cells and molecules, but by his own Spirit. By freely choosing death and going through it obediently to the end, he reversed the tragedy of all dying.

Having gone through it all, having finished the work that the Father gave him to do, John tells us, 'He bowed his head' as though to rest after labour. The word used can mean laying one's head gently on a pillow. There is a particularly poignant echo here, because our Lord had said of himself during the troubled years of his ministry, 'Foxes have holes and birds of the air have nests, but the Son of Man has no place to lay his head.' The word used here is the same word. He finally found where to lay his head – on the cross. This was his last act, his last word. He laid down his head and died. 'Father, into thy hands I commend my spirit.' This was the final free act of the only free man. By his act we are set free to seek after that same freedom.

PART 3

THE AFTERSHOCK

15 * Mystery

> But on the first day of the week, at early dawn,
> they went to the tomb, taking the spices which they
> had prepared. And they found the stone rolled away
> from the tomb, but when they went in they did not
> find the body. While they were perplexed about this,
> behold, two men stood by them in dazzling apparel;
> and as they were frightened and bowed their faces
> to the ground, the men said to them, 'Why do you
> seek the living among the dead?'
>
> (Luke 24.1–5, RSV)

Give or take a few repeats, and there have been
repeats, I've preached about twenty-five sermons
on the resurrection over the years. They seem
to fall into four categories. There are what I
think of as the court room sermons. In fact,
on one occasion I got a distinguished lawyer
to debate with me on the subject of the evidence for the resurrection in the sermon slot,
he arguing against it and I in favour. I won
the debate handsomely, probably because I'd
written both speeches. In my sermon files are
several utterances along the lines I adopted then,
rehearsing the cumulative case for treating the
resurrection as a provable historical fact on five
grounds.

The empty tomb: While it does not itself prove
anything it does show that something happened
to the body.

The appearances: The earliest account of these is 1 Corinthians, written probably about twenty years after the event itself. Against all expectation, the disciples, who had deserted him as a lost leader, have experiences, separately and together, that convince them Jesus, though dead, lives beyond death.

The new courage of the Apostles: The men who deserted him on Good Friday now proclaim their allegiance to him as a living Lord and endure suffering and death as a result. What changed them? They say the risen Jesus did.

The emergence of the Church: This same dispirited bunch of disciples finds a new and compelling message that persuades others to join them in a community which had the risen Jesus at its centre.

The experience of the Church down the ages that Jesus was, however mysteriously, a present fact, a contemporary experience, and not a dead hero.

Effectively or ineffectively, this group of sermons seeks to establish the resurrection as a fact of history, as well as a fact of faith, something as indisputably historical as the fall of the Berlin Wall in 1989. But another group of sermons takes a diametrically opposed point of view. To emphasize the allegedly historical or objective nature of the resurrection misses the whole point, I argued. The resurrection was not about something that happened to the dead body of Jesus; it was about something that happened to the living minds of his disciples. By some mystery of faith, the real meaning and message of Jesus finally clicked in their minds and hearts. Jesus rose in their understanding from the death of their own misinterpretation of him as a temporal, worldly leader to a true understanding of him as an eternal spiritual idea. The resurrection was something that happened to the disciples and they described this experience in the colourful language of metaphor: stones that rolled away from their closed minds, sudden illuminations, as they meditated on the meaning of Jesus, that came to them like angelic visitants. Alongside this impatience with an interpretation of the resurrection that was too literalistic went an exhortation to people that the important thing was not resurrection *then* but resurrection *now,* the experience of a living faith in the spirit and meaning of Jesus for our own day.

Then there is a third block of sermons that shows some impatience with each of these approaches. The resurrection is a mystery and there is no single way of interpreting it. People have to be allowed to approach it as they can. Literalists are not to force people into historical opinions about miracles they may not be able to hold in their minds. And metaphorists, who treat the resurrection as an unhistorical myth that conveys spiritual truth, should not be too dismissive of those who insist on treating it as a historical fact. How can they be so certain it isn't? Follow the principle of 'the available believable' — believe what is available to you and leave the rest for another time; the resurrection is a mountain that can be approached from different sides.

In more recent sermons I have noticed a preoccupation with the future. Interpretations of the resurrection that leave it in the past offend against its real genius. It is not essentially about the past at all, either a literal past or a metaphoric past. It is essentially about hope and hope is the future tense of faith. Resurrection faith is a radical trust in the power of God to come to us from the future. The past is no longer available to us except in our own memories, which subtly gild and edit it, making it more difficult for us to live in the present and look to the future. Politicians do it by so romanticizing their rosy vision of a vanished Britain that they fail to offer us appropriate guidance for our future in twenty-first-century Europe. We can fall into the same trap in the Church. We can be so obsessed with following God's directions for some people in their day that we fail to discern them for ourselves in our day. And the same can be true in our private experiences: guilt about the past or longing for the past can entomb us, unless God raises us to a living knowledge of forgiveness and a living experience of divine activity in our own day. Scripture and Christian experience teach us that grace is active in history, rolling away stones of guilt and oppression, bringing new illuminations, surprises. We have to be up early for such a God as Jesus described, a God who does new things and can open even our padlocked minds. Real faith in the resurrection would make us more daring and trusting; we wouldn't cling to old things, because we'd want our hands to be free to receive the new things God wants to give us.

For all their apparent contradictions and differences of emphasis, my struggles with the meaning of the resurrection, the central mystery of Christianity, have a certain consistency. We cannot ignore the accounts of the events in the New Testament, problematic as they are for the modern mind. We have to sit under them and listen, not by abandoning our twentieth-century consciousness but by bringing it with us to the work of understanding. And we are not arrogantly to decide that only one approach to the mystery will do. Even in a single life many approaches suggest themselves; even more will assert themselves in the lives of many. We ought to be modest before the mystery.

But the final word has to be about our own day. The resurrection is no resurrection for us if it is only about something that happened two thousand years ago – it is just another unresolved historical problem. The real testimony to the truth of this mystery is that it answers not only to our own heart's longing but to our own experience. There is hope as well as despair in life. Things pass away and we constantly lose what we love, but new things come to us, surprises keep us living. He is not here, we are constantly being told by the God of history, he is risen and has gone before us. We are not to look for him back there; we won't find the living among the dead; instead we are to go out into history, into God's great future and, if we are attentive, we shall see him turning the corner a pace or two ahead of us. And try as we might, we'll never catch up with him.

16 · Recognition

But Mary stood weeping outside the tomb, and as she wept she stooped to look into the tomb; and she saw two angels in white, sitting where the body of Jesus had lain, one at the head and one at the feet. They said to her, 'Woman, why are you weeping?' She said to them, 'Because they have taken away my Lord, and I do not know where they have laid him.' Saying this, she turned round and saw Jesus standing, but she did not know that it was Jesus. Jesus said to her, 'Woman, why are you weeping? Whom do you seek?' Supposing him to be the gardener, she said to him, 'Sir, if you have carried him away, tell me where you have laid him, and I will take him away.' Jesus said to her, 'Mary.' She turned and said to him in Hebrew, 'Rabboni!' (which means Teacher).

(John 20.11–16, RSV)

Years ago I read a story about a man who was falling out of love with his wife. He was finding the relationship stale and burdensome and began to dream about the possibility of a new love, the excitement of a new relationship. One day, having said goodbye to his wife and gone to his office, he looked out of the window and realized that it was spring. He decided to forsake the staff canteen and treat himself to lunch in a strange part of town. Towards the end of his meal he caught sight of a stunningly attractive woman on the street outside. Stung by loneliness and desire, he hurriedly paid his bill and rushed outside to follow her. Keeping a discreet distance, he tailed her for several blocks as she window-shopped, enjoying the warm spring day. 'I'm going to pick her up', he decided, 'Or try to – I can't let her simply disappear from my life.' And when she stopped to gaze into a shop window he drew near, his pulse racing, determined to accost her. As he opened his mouth to speak she turned and smiled warmly at him, and he found himself gazing with surprise at the face of his own wife.

That story irresistibly reminds me of the famous lines from 'Burnt Norton' by Eliot:

> We shall not cease from exploration
> And the end of all our exploring
> Will be to arrive where we started
> And know the place for the first time.

Familiarity blinds us to the significance, to the meaning and importance of a thing. There is something of this in our Lord's rueful comment that a prophet was not without honour save in his own country. I remember well the scene in the movie, *To Kill A Mockingbird,* where Gregory Peck, the gentle small-town lawyer, despised as boring and uninteresting by his young son, goes out to deal with a rabid dog that is terrorizing the neighbourhood. He stands alone in the street as the dog comes screaming towards him and calmly aims his rifle and kills it as it is about to leap. And we see a look of amazed reappraisal sweeping over the face of his contemptuous son. It sometimes takes a while for children to appreciate the significance of their parents and know them for the first time. Never to have known that sudden shock of recognition is life's greatest poverty. To have lost the ability to see the creation with surprise and wonder is life's greatest tragedy.

All of the great spiritual traditions try to train us to recover that ability to be amazed, to recognize the significance, the meaning, and depth of people and the natural world. Thomas Merton took up photography in his monastery in Kentucky so that he could practise the discipline of really looking at things and seeing them for the first time. And the contemplative use of Scripture has the same effect – looked at steadily and pondered slowly it yields up new meaning and we know it for the first time. Haste, knowingness, familiarity, and self pre-occupation are our greatest enemies – they insulate us from the shock of revelation, the newness of the familiar, the surprise of the accustomed.

And one of the strangest aspects of the resurrection story is the failure of his followers to recognize the risen Jesus. In John's Gospel, Mary Magdalene does not recognize Jesus and mistakes him for the gardener. Later in the Gospel, when Jesus meets his disciples on the shore of the Lake of Galilee, they take him for a friendly stranger. And this is also true of the famous and greatly loved story in Luke of the two disconsolate disciples whom the risen Jesus accompanies to Emmaus. In none of these cases is Jesus immediately recognized. This is a puzzling aspect of the tradition that's worth meditating on.

It suggests two things to me. The first is that, whatever the resurrection was, it wasn't the resuscitation of the dead body of Jesus. We are familiar with stories of such revivals in medical history today. Indeed, there is a new genre of literature: the post-mortem memoir. But people who are brought back from death by medical science or miracle are not resurrected. We describe them as being given a new lease on life, an extension, a bonus, a few more years. The experience may take away the fear of death, but it cannot take away death; that they will have to undergo again. That is not what happened to Jesus. His death was absolute and real. He was not raised from death, snatched from it just before its effects were irreversible, given another lease, an extension of the rental on his mortal body. He was raised beyond death into a different level of being. The accounts of his appearances stress this difference — the presence that confronted them was not immediately identifiable as the physical Jesus they had known. The recognition, when it occurred, was a shock. Mary made the connection when she heard him say her name; the disciples recognized him at Emmaus when he broke the bread; and at the end of John's Gospel, when he stands on the shore and calls out to his disciples who are fishing, it is the disciple whom Jesus loved who makes the connection. In each case they are yanked from their insulating self preoccupation and made to look at the mysterious stranger and see him for the first time, and they recognize, at last, not the physical manifestation, whatever that was, but the reality, the innerness, the identity of Jesus, the nature that had been transformed by God's action into a new creation – and they knew him for the first time.

But how was it done? How is our mind to grapple with this mystery? Recently I've been meditating on another mystery, the creation itself. I've always been haunted by the philosophers' question, 'Why is there anything at all and not just nothing?' Science is not able to answer why, but modern cosmology is able to take us back to the *when*, to the microsecond just after the birth of creation, the beginning of something and not just nothing: fifteen billion years and ten seconds ago – and the first ten seconds are unimaginably important – everything in the universe, all the matter that now composes billions of stars and billions of galaxies, was an incredibly dense mass, so small it could pass through the eye of a needle. From that point it expanded very rapidly and at only three minutes from zero most of the main elements of the universe were formed. The expansion in the first ten seconds was so rapid and so violent that astronomers coined the phrase 'the Big Bang' to help us think about it. Fifteen billion years later, the universe, which is still expanding, achieved consciousness in us and started asking questions about itself. How are we to grapple with this mystery? Before the discoveries of the new science we had a picture of the universe as a great machine, solid, material, predictable, without beginning and without end. Now we know we had a beginning in a density of explosive nothingness from which everything else has evolved. This is what Stephen Hawking means by the mind of God. We come from nothing, some would say or, as others might put it, from nothing but the mind of God. If from that nothingness we were called into existence; if from that nothingness came the galaxies and the great corridors of space; if from that nothingness came beauty and holiness, prayer and music, art and literature, and all the strange passions of humanity; why should it be thought impossible that the God of the galaxies could not inaugurate a new creation from the emptiness of the death of his servant Jesus? 'Why is there something and not just nothing?' I don't know exactly, but I believe it is because the eternal God said 'Let there be', and there was something.

Why did the disciples, broken and defeated, tell the world they had seen the Lord, and would die rather than deny it? I don't know exactly, but I believe it was because the Eternal God inaugurated a new creation, a new dimension of reality, a new universe, with its own laws of being, in the person of his faithful servant Jesus. But it is so close to us we don't recognize it, so familiar that it has lost its power to surprise us. Maybe it's time we trailed Jesus like an attractive stranger to see if he will turn and smile at us.

17 * *The Enduring Surprise*

> Jesus said to her, 'Do not hold me, for I have not yet ascended to the Father; but go to my brethren and say to them, I am ascending to my Father and your Father, to my God and your God.' Mary Magdalene went and said to the disciples, 'I have seen the Lord'; and she told them that he had said these things to her.
>
> (John 20.17–18, RSV)

Sometimes the absence of a loved one seems to be more powerful than her presence. As my children left home, one by one, I would enter their rooms and try to touch the memories of their childhood and bring them back to mind. I knew a widow who kept her husband's chair exactly the way it was the night he died, with his half-smoked pipe still lying in the ashtray on a table beside it. Even whole cities can powerfully suggest the absence of one we love. A great friend of mine from Boston in the USA died a few years ago and when I visit Boston I am overwhelmingly aware of his absence. The place seems empty, like the tomb Mary Magdalene found when she came seeking Jesus on the first day of the week.

Of course, we only know the absence of someone who was once present, once known and loved and now missed intensely. There is another experience of loss that is much more difficult to account for. There are certain places that evoke a sort of nostalgia for something we've never known. Holy places, for instance, can have this effect, even for unbelievers. They suggest a presence even though the place is empty. Mysteriously, many people sense the absence of God in this way. They have never known God, may not believe in God, yet they miss God's presence, sense the absence of something. But how can we feel bereft of something that never was? The very longing for God, the sense of being without God, is powerful testimony to the reality of God. How can we miss so piercingly, long for so passionately, someone who never existed? The sun may go into eclipse but we know it is there behind the cloud. It is hard to understand why it should be so, but it is the testimony of the saints that God is never closer to us than when we feel only God's absence.

Maybe human experience of loss can teach us something here. It is true that we lose our children as children but it's an even keener joy to get them back as adult friends. Even mourning for dead loved ones can be mysteriously transmuted into gratitude for the life they had. The yogis tell us that God can fill only the empty cup. If we wait patiently before the absences in our life new meaning will fill them, the way the risen Jesus replaced the earthly Jesus for the disciples.

Recently, I've been meditating on how people change their minds about things, embrace new ideas, adopt new attitudes. I've changed my mind about many things down the years.

Cardinal Newman said that 'growth was the only evidence of life' and 'to be perfect will be to have changed often.' Strange, therefore, how some people pride themselves on the fixity of their beliefs. They are the kind of people who boast that they won't believe in such-and-such even though one were to rise from the dead in front of their very eyes. It's easy to overlook what we don't want to see. To see or hear a new thing we have to be open-minded, ready for surprises.

We find new ideas difficult or uncongenial because we have grown fond of the old ones; we cherish and cling to the things that have been important to us. Loyalty of this sort is an important element in human faithfulness but it can also be a trap. It can keep us from growing morally and spiritually by trapping us in the past. There would have been no development in human history if human beings in the past had refused absolutely to entertain a new idea. Human institutions are like cars, they need accelerators as well as brakes. An African priest living in Britain observed recently that the Church in Britain was a most peculiar machine, because it had the engine of a lawnmower and the brakes of a juggernaut.

When new ideas, new approaches to things, new discoveries about human nature come to us, they come to us from outside our experience, and challenge us to change. They invite us to examine our attitudes, ask us why we cling to what we know, and are never prepared to look afresh at something that has, perhaps, been confronting us for years. That is the way many people are in their attitude towards the ministry of women. They simply refuse to look at it as a challenge that might be coming from God. They do not believe God can come to us from the future. The God they worship is tethered firmly to the past.

But some things take a while to dawn on us. The hardest wood takes longest to grow. Sometimes the loves that endure best took longest to develop. And there is a strange mercy in the slow triumph over adversity. I'm always moved by the knowledge that two of the greatest orators in twentieth-century Britain struggled against speech impediments — Winston Churchill and Aneurin Bevan. Because there were certain words he found hard to pronounce, the young Bevan learned synonyms he could pronounce – and greatly expanded his vocabulary in the process. Slowly overcoming difficulties can create great strength of character. Wrestling honestly and long with a new idea before blessing it can produce passionate commitment. Katherine Charnley puts it well:

> Strange how grit
> should turn to gift,
> and yet it is so.

Some resurrections
are slow:

not easily won
but worked
from difficult stone.

(Glass and Stone, p. 18)

That is why it is tragic when people become so personally invested in an idea that they are not able
to hear it challenged. The truth is never afraid of
being tested. If it is found to be wrong then it is
no longer truth and what takes its place is the new
truth we must follow. Truth in any area is not
easily won. What matters is that we shall want to
know the truth even if it upsets all our preconcep-
tions. Christians have often been bad at this, slow
to adjust to new knowledge in case it made them
disloyal to Jesus. Simone Weil once said that if it
ever comes to a choice between Jesus and truth we
must always choose truth, because disloyalty to
truth will always prove, in the long run, to have
been disloyalty to Jesus. This also is part of the surprise and newness of the resurrection. It calls us to
a life of joyful struggle.

Mary Magdalene had to learn not to cling to the
Jesus she had known in the past. She had to surrender that loyalty in order to discover the new
reality of the risen Jesus. It is only when we cease
to cling to experiences, realities, relationships that
have had their day, that we can move into and live
in the future. The resurrection teaches us that God

is God of the future as well as the past. This is why Christianity has been a revolutionary agent in human history. It has given people hope for their own lives: they have learned that loss is often the prelude to new discovery, new deepening of trust. They have been taught by the resurrection that the God of surprises is waiting for them beyond loss, beyond death, and nothing can keep us from the shock of his love.